RESTORING
the REPUBLIC

RESTORING *the* REPUBLIC

A CLEAR, CONCISE, AND COLORFUL BLUEPRINT FOR AMERICA'S FUTURE

DEVIN NUNES

WND Books

Restoring the Republic

WND Books

Published by WorldNetDaily

Washington, D.C.

WND Books are distributed to the trade by:
Midpoint Trade Books
27 West 20th Street, Suite 1102
New York, NY 10011

WND Books are available at special discounts for bulk purchases. WND Books, Inc. also publishes books in electronic formats. For more information call (541) 474-1776 or visit www.wndbooks.com.

First Edition

ISBN 13 Digit: 978-1-935071-19-8

Library of Congress information available

Printed in the United States of America

*To Elizabeth, Evelyn, and Julia for making
the sacrifices that allow me to serve, and to the people
of the great San Joaquin valley for making it possible.*

TABLE OF CONTENTS

INTRODUCTION

THOMAS JEFFERSON SAID IN 1807, A LITTLE OVER THREE DECADES after the founding of the United States:

> *We are a people capable of self-government, and worthy of it.*[1]

Jefferson was a great republican—against monarchy and big government, and for freedom and the rights of everyday people. He believed the people, not politicians and bureaucrats, should be the source of power in a republic. As Jefferson observed in 1797:

> *It was by the sober sense of our citizens that we were safely and steadily conducted from monarchy to republicanism, and it is by the same agency alone we can be kept from falling back.*[2]

What would Jefferson think of our government today? Probably very little. The Democrats, and even some Republicans, are a lot like Jefferson's bitter rivals, the Federalists, who supported a powerful central government, weaker states, and diminished individual freedom. And like the Federalists, Democrats today promote the interests of the banks and big business; they stand up for the fat cats even more than Republicans are accused of doing. Moreover, the Democrats have betrayed Jefferson's legacy by making their party the home of the radical left, which pursues an authoritarian agenda that has little in common with Jeffersonian democracy.

This is where the real threat to our Republic lies: the convergence of big government, big business, and the radical left in Washington.

Much of the threat stems from the environmental lobby, which forms a major component of the radical left. I became an outspoken critic of this lobby after witnessing first-hand the damage it has wreaked in my home state of California, from devastating man-made droughts to job-killing regulations. Although many environmentalists simply want to responsibly preserve our natural heritage (indeed most Americans, including myself, would count as environmentalists in this sense), these are not the people who control the environmental lobby—those powerful, well-funded interest groups that pursue an anti-capitalist, anti-economic growth, and anti-democratic agenda that aims to bring about a green utopia. In fact, economically ruinous green policies have turned the region I come from, the San Joaquin Valley, into the country's main battleground between commonsense local residents and environmental extremists.

As a congressman, I've had my share of dealings with this lobby, but one meeting stands out in my memory. In spring 2009, the Environmental Defense Fund (EDF) invited me to a reception in the historic Senate Russell Caucus Room, an ornate space that has been witness to the Army-McCarthy, Watergate, and Iran–Contra hearings. Despite the hardship the radical environmentalists have inflicted on my constituents and my entire state, the EDF apparently thought they could win me over; such is the silly utopian world in which they live.

At the reception, one EDF member explained cap and trade to me as a "market-based" solution to global warming. Of course, in reality cap and trade is a radical, convoluted scheme to foist what is effectively a giant tax increase on all Americans. The policy is supported by the environmental lobby, big business, and proponents of big government, all of whom will benefit from the resulting tax dollars and government regulation. I was surprised the guy assumed his slippery free-market sales pitch would convince me to support one of the most economically destructive proposals I've ever seen in Congress.

That annoying conversation was weird enough, but then I saw something *really* strange: a person who didn't belong in the room.

I suddenly recalled a childhood memory: after my parents went to sleep, my brother and I would sneak out of bed and watch *The Twilight Zone*. I grew up in the countryside of the San Joaquin Valley, where there are more cows than people, miles of fields that grow over 300 crops, and at the time only five channels on broadcast TV: ABC, NBC, the local station, PBS (the government-run station that, in typical government fashion, stopped broadcasting late at night), and CBS, which aired

The Twilight Zone. What I saw brought to mind Rod Serling's classic introduction to the show:

> *You unlock this door with the key of imagination. Beyond*
> *it is another dimension—a dimension of sound, a dimension*
> *of sight, a dimension of mind. You're moving into a land of*
> *both shadow and substance, of things and ideas. You've just*
> *crossed over into the Twilight Zone.*

The person I saw was Hank Paulson, the former Treasury Secretary under President George W. Bush. I had heard rumors

Companies Allied with Extremist Groups

Big Business Finance

AES Corp.
Alcoa Inc.
Alstom
Boston Scientific Corp.
Chrysler LLC
Deere and Co.
Dow Chemical Co.
Duke Energy Corp.
DuPont Co.
Exelon Corp.
Ford Motor Co.
FPL Group
General Electric Co.
General Motors Corp.
Honeywell International Inc.
Johnson and Johnson

NRG Energy Inc.
Pacific Gas and Electric Co.
PepsiCo Inc.
PNM Resources Inc.
Rio Tinto Group
Royal Dutch Shell
Siemens Corp.
Weyerhaeuser Co.
Green Beneficiaries

Green Activism

The Nature Conservancy
World Resources Institute
Natural Resources Defense Council
Pew Center on Global Climate Change
Environmental Defense Fund

This coalition of large U.S. companies and radical environmental groups have formed an alliance known as the U.S. Climate Action Partnership. Environmentalists and their corporate allies both stand to make money from global warming fear-mongering, including income from massive amounts of government spending. (Source: U.S. Climate Action Partnership) that Paulson was tied to the environmental lobby, and here he was in the flesh—a real Wall Street fat cat, the former chairman of Goldman Sachs, and an honored guest at a reception hosted by the Environmental Defense Fund. Only later did I learn that when Paulson had run Goldman Sachs, the firm gained a valuable tract of 680,000 acres of forest in Chile. Abandoning a plan to create a wood harvesting operation to pull in an estimated $150 million in annual revenues, Goldman simply donated the land to the Wildlife Conservation Society—where Paulson's son served as a trustee.[3] Paulson has also donated his own money to radical green groups like the League of Conservation Voters Action Fund, a key member of the environmental lobby.[4]

Paulson, with his questionable business deals and his hobnobbing with the EDF, stands at the nexus between big business, big government, and radical leftwing groups. But other examples aren't hard to find. We've seen it with big oil companies collaborating with the environmental lobby to promote "green jobs"; with Wal-Mart supporting radical healthcare reform; and with carmakers being taken over by the federal government.

Furthermore, during the 2008 banking crisis, we heard Paulson, some other Republicans, and virtually all Democratic leaders effectively declare that certain banks and businesses were too big to fail—if they went bankrupt, the economy would plunge into a depression and Americans would be financially ruined. Well, that's what they *said*, but what they *meant* was that certain banks and corporations (including Goldman Sachs) must not be allowed to fail because of their close relationship to the federal government and to influential politicians.

Democrats may be competing hard with Republicans to be the standard bearer for big business, but the truth is, big business doesn't care who's in charge, because it has successfully co-opted both parties. And notwithstanding leftist anti-corporate rhetoric, big business frequently teams up with radical leftwing groups, which can be bought off and even turned into allies.

The conditions brought about by the convergence of big business, big government, and the radical left have provoked hundreds of thousands of Americans to protest at tea party rallies. These everyday folks want real solutions instead of what they see coming out of Washington today. It is their tax dollars that go to bail out politically connected big businesses, and they don't understand where they fit in a political system that caters to corporations deemed "too big to fail."

This book is not intended as a defense of the Republican Party's recent actions; after all, it was a Republican administration that ushered in our new bailout culture. Instead, this book aims to illuminate a path forward for Americans who are frustrated with their government in Washington, D.C., and who are desperately seeking a way to restore the vitality and fiscal stability of our Republic. It will also outline policies and legislation designed to renew the Republican Party, because Republicans are the only champions of limited government and individual freedom, even if the party doesn't always live up to its ideals. My hope is that Republicans will again be inspired by Jefferson to become "republican" in the truest sense of the word. Democrats, in contrast, are hopelessly compromised by their support for big government and their intimate connections to the radical left.

What's really too big to fail? Our Republic is too big to fail. It has been too important, for too long, to too many people. Without it, the world would be darker and less free. When British colonial subjects staked their lives, liberty, and property on building a republic in America, they also intended future generations of Americans to do their part to maintain it.

When the Founding Fathers cut their bonds to the British monarchy, they had little reason to hope for success. No previous republic in history had survived. And if they failed, most would likely have been executed.

Yet our Republic has endured. It's an historic achievement enabled by successive generations of Americans who have courageously protected and defended it. But we could fail, if Americans should ever lose the courage that originated in those thirteen daring colonies.

As Thomas Jefferson said in 1787:

> *I am not discouraged by [a] little difficulty; nor have I any doubt that the result of our experiment will be, that men are capable of governing themselves without a master.*[5]

CHAPTER ONE

REFLECTIONS

"Who will mow the lawns?"
—Devin Nunes

ONE DAY IN AUTUMN 2008, I WAS SITTING IN THE U.S. CAPITOL
with several high-ranking Treasury Department officials who were
lobbying Congress to bail out Wall Street. Under their proposal—
then called the Paulson Plan, now known as the Troubled Asset
Relief Program (TARP)—the government would buy up banks'
toxic assets and supposedly sell them later for a profit. They told
me without this action, the banking system would fail, the stock
market would plunge, and the economy would collapse. There was
no time for debate, I was warned; Congress had to act now. Those
of us delaying the plan by asking inconvenient questions would
allegedly be responsible for another Great Depression.

The doomsday rhetoric was insulting to the intelligence of the
American people. In a C-SPAN interview, I called these threats

the legislative equivalent of "breaking arms." Unfortunately, I was pretty lonely back then in my opposition to the scheme. The vast majority of our nation's leaders, both Democrats and Republicans, succumbed to the hysteria and supported the bailouts.

During that autumn meeting, I listened quietly to all the nonsense justifying passage of a bill nobody had read. I was thinking about the practical, everyday effects in my district of the government buying up reams of bad mortgages. Then I spoke:

"If you can answer one question for me, I will support your bailout."

An impatient Treasury official snapped, *"What's the question, Congressman?"*

I looked him in the eye and asked, *"When the government buys up these bad loans and takes ownership of empty houses in my district, who will mow the lawns?"*

The Treasury experts looked at me like I was speaking a foreign language. Clearly perturbed by the question, they confessed, *"We don't know."*

So I told them, *"I won't be voting for your bill, then. And by the way, don't buy any houses in my district. I don't want calls from constituents on weekends asking me to come over and mow the lawn of the empty government-owned house next door."*

"But if you don't vote for this, there will be a run on the banks," they insisted.

Finally, I had a glimmer of hope. Smiling, I told the officials, *"Now you've said something that makes sense. That's a problem we can solve."* To protect people's life savings and shore up the banks, I proposed increasing the Federal Deposit Insurance Corporation (FDIC) limits. After being informed that around 100 banks were in trouble, I further suggested that the Federal Reserve offer temporary loans to those banks that had a chance of survival.

Regarding me as a fool, they replied, *"We would never do that, Congressman."*

Eleven days later, the Treasury did just that—but they did a whole lot more, too. Unimpressed by my restrained proposals, they took an extreme course, buying preferred shares in troubled banks and offering bailout money to any bank in America. They even pressured some banks that didn't want bailouts to take them anyway, in order to avoid stigmatizing the others. In the case of Citibank, the Treasury went further and bought common stock, making the government a co-owner of a major bank.

I remember October 3, 2008, the day TARP passed the House. I was with two other Republican members of Congress standing on the Speaker's balcony overlooking the Washington Mall. It's a magnificent view, the eye drifting down the long expanse of the Mall, past the Washington Monument to the Lincoln Memorial. The three of us had been successful as a whip team in generating opposition to the first TARP bill a few days earlier, defeating it by a slender thirteen votes. But our victory was short lived. On October 3, a second TARP bill was sent to Congress, and this time it passed. I felt sick to my stomach.

"It's over," I said to Michigan's Thaddeus McCotter and Steve LaTourette of Ohio. We had all just stepped off the House floor following the intense pressure put on members of Congress during the second TARP vote.

"What are you talking about?" McCotter asked.

"The American economy. The big banks have just become a department of the U.S. government," I replied.

"You're right, beater," Thad said.

Steve and I looked at each other perplexed. Finally Steve asked, *"What the heck is a beater?"*

McCotter explained, *"In India, when Queen Victoria's son Edward wanted to hunt tigers, he would say, 'Summon the beaters.' Beaters would beat the bushes to stir the tigers. The problem was that the beater was either shot by the hunter or eaten by a tiger."*

Knowing McCotter, I waited for the punch line. *"Today,"* he said, *"we have been shot by the hunter and eaten by the tiger!"*

I knew what he meant—we were the beaters, tramping through the political wilderness on a doomed mission to stop the growth of government. Congress approved TARP in a bipartisan panic attack, thereby transferring unprecedented constitutional duties to the executive branch and paying nearly $1 trillion for the privilege. America had been put on a path to the large-scale nationalization of private industry, a new system where politicians and bureaucrats would run the economy from Washington, D.C. The outcome was perhaps best characterized by a *Newsweek* cover proclaiming, "We are all socialists now."

Political leaders from both parties fueled hysteria and sped passage of the flawed Wall Street bailout bill through the Democrat-controlled Congress. (Photo by Mark Wilson, Getty Images News)

As more information about the injustices, inefficiencies, and corruption of the bailouts has come to light, the number of bailout critics has grown. Many congressmen now understand Congress's foolishness in granting unprecedented authority to the Treasury with no strings attached. Yet those who now complain the loudest in both parties are often the very legislators who created TARP. They had a responsibility to lead our nation in a time of crisis, and they failed.

There is now incontrovertible evidence the bailouts were a reckless failure. Despite the promise to save 100 banks, in 2009 133 banks went out of business. Additionally, the 2010 FDIC budget increased by $1.4 billion to handle even more bank failures; although the biggest, most well-connected banks were saved from their own irresponsible decisions at taxpayer expense, apparently someone decided that not all banks were "too big to fail."

In late 2009, Secretary Paulson's bailout point-man, Neel Kashkari, told a *Washington Post* reporter how he conjured TARP's exorbitant price tag:

> Seven hundred billion was a number out of the air. It was a political calculus. I said, "We don't know how much is enough. We need as much as we can get [from Congress]. What about a trillion?" No way, Hank shook his head. I said, "Okay, what about $700 billion?" We didn't know if it would work. We had to project confidence, hold up the world. We couldn't admit how scared we were, or how uncertain.[1]

To my horror, our nation's leaders didn't stop there. The American taxpayer was taken on a bailout ride, propping up banks that should have failed, rescuing foreign banks and foreign firms with U.S. tax dollars, and even taking ownership of financial companies and car companies. It was almost beyond belief—a socialist renaissance not in Europe or the former Soviet states, but in America.

As I sat in that room listening to the Treasury gurus, my mind drifted back to the summer of 1990, when I was sixteen. I was delivering irrigation water to a dehydrated corn crop in California's San Joaquin Valley. My family worked as tenant farmers back then, and we had rented some land that was running short on water. So we had to rent a well from a local farmer to save our crops. The water had to be moved a quarter mile up hill, which caused the ditch leading from the well continually to crack. This meant a lot of dirt shoveling in sweltering, 100-plus degree heat.

One afternoon I was patching a break in the ditch, and up drove a shiny, new, white pickup truck. Out stepped a man who informed me he was from the local mosquito abatement department.

"You can't leave water on the ground like that," he said. *"It attracts mosquitoes."*

"No kidding!" I said. *"I'm trying to stop it."*

"Well, you have to fix it now," he informed me.

"What do you think I'm doing?" I asked. *"Why don't you go get a shovel out of the back of my truck and help? If not, get out of my way."*

He quickly returned to his truck and sped away. It was my first real encounter with the government. Here I was, trying to stop water from flowing out of the ditch—after all, my family had paid for the water—and I sure didn't need the government wasting my time stating the obvious.

From the local mosquito abatement department to the U.S. Treasury Department, not much had changed. I had gone from one big, burdensome, and bureaucratic department to another. Both like to take power away from individuals and give it to politicians and bureaucrats—people who have no idea what it's like to live in the real world or what the problems of everyday people are like.

One thing never changes about big government: it costs a lot of money. And the bailouts were just the beginning. They were followed by a healthcare reform bill that gobbles up one-sixth of the U.S. economy, creating over 100 new federal bodies and programs to force a ream of new regulations on Americans and American businesses, including the intrusive mandate that all Americans buy health insurance.[2] With our national financial health already eroding fast, the Democrats created a massive new entitlement that can only be financially justified through blatant accounting gimmicks like double counting, raising taxes years before benefits are increased in order to lower the bill's short-term cost, and others.

The Obama administration's stated price tag for the bill—just under $1 trillion—is the stuff of pure fantasy. According to the Heritage Foundation, once you discount the budgeting tricks, "the true 10-year cost of this bill is at least $2.5 trillion."[3] Even Obama's own Health and Human Services Department reported in April 2010, just a month after the healthcare bill passed, that the bill was more likely to raise spending over the next ten years than reduce the deficit, as the Democrats had promised. The report also found it was doubtful that $500 billion in Medicare cuts, which was supposed to be a key source for funding the bill, would be sustained.[4]

Politicians promising entitlements they can't actually pay for? What a shock.

The government is spending us into oblivion as it takes more and more power away from the individual. America now stands at a crossroads. One road, the road outlined in this book, will empower the individual and restore our Republic. The other road, the road we're now on, will lead to financial ruin.

Our country is headed for disaster because our current level of government spending is unsustainable. To finance the spending, we'll have to print money and borrow from foreigners and foreign governments. In five years, this will accumulate $15 trillion in debt, an amount larger than our GDP today.

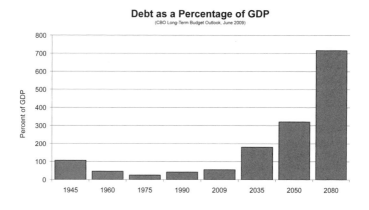

Debt as a Percentage of GDP
(CBO Long-Term Budget Outlook, June 2009)

As large as this number seems, however, it's small compared to the full U.S. debt—the financial obligations ignored by Congress. Indeed, our nation has amassed tens of trillions of dollars in unfunded liabilities in Medicare, Medicaid, and Social Security. This fact has been well documented by annual Treasury reports and by independent actuaries responsible for advising Congress on our long-term budget commitments. Nevertheless, our government leaders continue to speed along a one-way road to bankruptcy.

In this book, you will read about solutions to big problems—solutions that focus on stabilizing our nation's finances and empowering individuals to live their lives free from government meddling. The reforms recommended here seek to reward individual responsibility and initiative—the values that have always enriched America. Indeed, all these proposals assume that success in America is achieved not by a government guarantee, but by hard work, a drive to innovate, and a spirit of entrepreneurship.

The United States has nurtured reliance on family, friends, and neighbors—not government. When individuals need the assistance of government, however, they turn to their town, county, or state government—in that order. Few Americans see the vast, remote, and impenetrable bureaucracy in Washington, D.C., as a solution to their problems.

Empowering individuals is not a slogan. It's a way to achieve practical solutions to problems affecting everyday people. Who are everyday people? They are not politicians and bureaucrats, but the people who pay their salaries, like you (and me, before I was elected to Congress). They work hard, feed their families, pay their mortgages, drive their kids to soccer practice, pay for college, and are active in their local communities. Everyday people look to government to provide basic services and to protect them "against all enemies, foreign and domestic." They don't need advice from the government on how to live their lives, and they sure don't want the government to give their hard-earned tax dollars to well-connected special interests or freeloaders. A Portuguese immigrant friend said it best:

I have two cows, and the government lets me keep one and makes me give the other to someone who doesn't work."

Politicians often merely complain and demagogue instead of offering practical solutions to the problems we face. And so nothing gets done; or worse, government gets bigger, Washington grows more powerful, and still the problems grow worse. Either way, everyday people lose. It's time politicians proposed concrete, practical solutions or, just like the mosquito abatement guy, get out of the way.

This book will recommend actual legislation before Congress that will improve the lives of everyday people. I especially support "A Roadmap for America's Future," which proposes reforms to entitlements, taxes, and healthcare, as well as "A Roadmap for America's Energy Future," which sets out energy reforms. I will explain the problems and then offer solutions, focusing on the most important issues. Many dominate the headlines. When they don't, there's usually a reason. That's why I lead off the book with redistricting; no one talks about redistricting because it's a dirty little secret politicians don't want you to know about.

Then come the headline grabbers: how we can break free from foreign oil and achieve energy independence; the "big three"—Medicare, Medicaid, and Social Security—which stand to bankrupt America if they aren't dealt with swiftly; real tax reform for hard-working Americans; immigration, the issue loved by demagogues but rarely dealt with seriously; and education, where we can improve the performance of our students and reduce the federal government's meddling in our schools.

I will finish with American foreign policy and our place in the world. This relates to the aforementioned problems, for if we don't solve them, the United States will be severely weakened—perhaps permanently. This would not only afflict Americans, but it would demoralize billions of other souls who look to our country as a land where the ideals of "life, liberty, and the pursuit of happiness" project hope to dark, impoverished parts of the world.

CHAPTER TWO

REDISTRICTING

"Those who have refused to pay?
God help them!"
—U.S. Representative from California

BACKGROUND

REDISTRICTING IS THE PROCESS BY WHICH DISTRICTS ARE DRAWN
to elect the House of Representatives. Mandated by the
Constitution every ten years based on the census, redistricting
requires the division of every state into voting districts with similar numbers of residents to insure the "one man, one vote" rule.

PROBLEM

If you asked the average citizen to name the twenty issues most
important to him or her, redistricting probably wouldn't even
make the list. Indeed, many Americans have never even heard the
term, much less spent any time worrying about it. And that's just
the way the politicians want it.

Here's why this little-known issue is the key to restoring our Republic: there is a long-standing bipartisan conspiracy to subvert American democracy. It plays out when politicians meet behind closed doors to draw the boundaries of their voting districts. These borders are routinely drawn to protect incumbents, both Democrats and Republicans, from facing competitive elections. Gerrymandering, as this underhanded process is called, is a deliberate corruption of our political system. Instead of voters choosing their politicians, politicians are choosing their voters. You, the voter, are merely part of an incumbent protection program.

Gerrymandering is nothing new. But that doesn't make the farce any more tolerable. There isn't much public discussion of this issue because neither party raises it; both Democratic and Republican incumbents have a vested interest in perpetuating the current system. But ending this sham and imposing accountability on our representatives is crucial to securing this country's future. With their power safely protected by rigged voting contests, many congressmen have become dangerously disconnected from the people they supposedly represent. I consider this the most pressing issue today because Congress's votes on all other issues, on both foreign and domestic policy, will be wiser, more responsible, and more practical once our representatives are made truly accountable to the American people.

"Gerrymandering" is named after Elbridge Gerry, a Massachusetts governor who signed an 1812 redistricting bill that gave Jefferson's Democratic-Republican Party an edge in the state senate. A redrawn district was said to look like a salamander, and Gerry's name was added to form a new term, "gerrymandering," that refers to convoluted electoral boundaries drawn for partisan reasons.

The legislative districts depicted in the above *Boston Sentinel* cartoon were created by the Massachusetts legislature in 1812.

By the way, not much has changed in Massachusetts. In the southern part of the state, there are roughly 300,000 Portuguese-Americans, many whose families have lived there for generations. But Massachusetts has never elected an American of Portuguese descent to Congress. This is by design; each decade the politicians in Boston draw the districts to dilute the influence of the Portuguese-American community. As a result, Americans of Irish descent dominate the Bay State's congressional delegation, while Portuguese-Americans are sliced and diced into several districts.

The redistricting process is manipulated just about everywhere, including in my home state of California. In 2001, the California legislature did a bipartisan gerrymander that would have made old Gerry proud. Democrats and Republicans jointly drew safe seats to insure that all incumbents would be easily re-elected. The scheme was so successful, in fact, that only one incumbent in California's fifty-three congressional districts has lost in nearly a decade.

That unlikely loser was Republican Richard Pombo. Why? He tried to reform the Endangered Species Act, which the environmental lobby exploits to bring devastating lawsuits designed to stop nearly all forms of manufacturing, energy production, and economic growth. In response, the lobby launched what the *Wall Street Journal*'s Kimberley Strassel called "the most coordinated, expensive attack in their political history."[1] Environmental groups spent millions on scurrilous attack ads, coordinating their campaign from newly opened offices in Pombo's district. Activists harassed him and his wife at their ranch and even followed his children to school, Pombo told me. Helped by a convenient gerrymander, the greens defeated him. The lesson here is that well-funded special interests can still defeat incumbents, but grassroots citizens have little chance.

Gerrymandering has become a crucial part of politicians' campaigns. Democrats paid a redistricting consultant $1.36 million to draw California's districts after the 2000 census.[2] In a shocking moment of honesty, one southern California Democrat admitted:

Twenty thousand [dollars] is nothing to keep your seat. I spend $2 million (campaigning) every year. If my colleagues are smart, they'll pay their $20,000 and [the redistricting consultant] will draw the district they can win in. Those who have refused to pay? God help them![3]

California's 23rd district is a classic example of gerrymandering. It stretches nearly 300 miles from north to south and is only about five miles wide. In fact, at high tide parts of the district actually disappear into the Pacific. By any measure, its inhabitants have little in common other than a beautiful coastline and a high likelihood of voting for a Democrat. The district is particularly safe for incumbents because it's spread over five different media markets, meaning challengers would need to spend well over $5 million just to introduce themselves to all the voters.

The 23rd Congressional District is a classic example of gerrymandering. As seen here, the district stretches 300 miles north to south and is only five miles wide.

Today's gerrymandered congressmen are like old European royals (the same kind early Americans escaped from), who knew they could never survive free and fair elections. District boundaries are now the equivalent of castle walls, protected by motes and drawbridges, keeping all challengers out. It's quite the opposite of what the Founders envisioned for America, where the House of Representatives would be the people's house, accountable to the voters every two years.

The people have been locked out of the electoral process without even knowing it. In a January 2010 interview, C-SPAN president Brian Lamb spoke eloquently about the outrageous way politicians avoid accountability and transparency. Although he was speaking about congressional Democrats' refusal to allow TV coverage of their negotiations on healthcare reform, his sentiments could easily apply to the corrupt, backroom wheeling and dealing of the redistricting process:

> We obviously would cover these negotiations. The only time we've been allowed to cover the White House part of it is one hour inside the East Room, which was just a show-horse type of thing.
>
> ... The American people pay for all of this that goes on in [Washington]. It's always been my contention... that if we pay for something, and it's the public's business, we ought to be able to see how it's done. It's just that simple, it has nothing to do with this particular fight right now.[4]

SOLUTION

The good news about gerrymandering is that Congress, if it had the will, could stop it pretty easily by imposing tough rules on the drawing of voting districts. These rules must require states to limit the number of times counties and cities are sliced and stuffed into different districts. This limitation would force politicians to serve people who actually live in the same neighborhoods and communities; go to the same schools, churches, and football games; and use the same roads and businesses.

Recently, some politicians have almost completely disappeared from their districts in order to avoid their constituents' tough questions about their votes for stimulus bills, bank bailouts, and the government's increasing intrusion into the private sector. It's unlikely we'd see that anymore after redistricting reform, since politicians would become genuinely accountable to the people, who would finally get a real choice on Election Day.

If Congress won't pass tough guidelines in time for the current round of redistricting, it can surely do it before the next census in 2020. This simple step is probably the single most effective way to restore the people's faith in Congress.

CHAPTER THREE

ENERGY

*"12 to 32 animals would be removed,
lured to their deaths by recorded calls and
an owl decoy, then shot at close range."*
—Associated Press

BACKGROUND

AMERICANS HAVE BUILT THE WORLD'S MOST SUCCESSFUL ECON-
omy, in part because we have effectively developed and used
cheap, abundant energy sources. As a result, Americans, with 4.5
percent of the world's population, consume a little over 20 percent
of the world's energy supplies and produce 20 percent of the
world's GDP. Throughout our history, as more powerful energy
sources have become available, we have used them to increase our
productivity. This in turn has increased our standard of living.

Over 80 percent of our energy comes from fossil fuels—mainly
oil, natural gas, and coal—and there are no immediate alternatives

for them.[1] Although "green" energy is much touted these days, less than 1 percent of our energy comes from solar and wind power.[2]

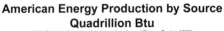

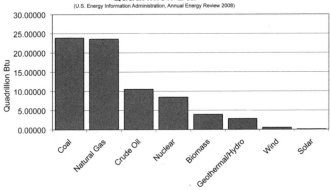

Despite billions in federal research spending, generous tax credits for consumers and manufactures, and punitive taxes and regulations related to fossil fuel production, coal, natural gas, and crude oil remain the backbone of American energy. (U.S. Energy Information Administration, Annual Energy Review 2008)

PROBLEM

America needs to boost its energy security—that is, we need to increase our access to a stable, affordable energy supply to power our economy. For decades, our government has mismanaged energy policy, spending billions on "alternative" forms of energy. Yet our energy outlook continues to deteriorate, and energy prices constantly rise. In fact, U.S. dependence on foreign oil is much greater now than it was in 1977, when President Jimmy Carter described our energy challenges as the "moral equivalent of war."

Free market advocates, including me, have long argued that government policies are damaging America's energy security. We believe restrictive laws, excessive regulations, and high taxes have driven U.S. energy development overseas and artificially raised prices. Although the United States has the biggest projected energy supplies in the world, vast areas are not accessible on government lands.[3] In fact, 97 percent of government offshore lands are not even being explored for energy, and onshore, 94 percent remain unleased.[4]

The group that keeps this energy off-limits is the environmental lobby. One of the most powerful and well-funded special interests in Washington today, this lobby intimidates many politicians into adopting extreme positions prohibiting almost any energy development. Other politicians share the lobby's goal of bringing about an expensive, limited, and rationed energy supply as a way to increase centralized government control over the economy. For example, many insist the only solution to our foreign oil dependence is to develop solar panels and windmills, even though they know these alternatives can't come close to replacing fossil fuels in our energy mix.

The environmental lobby attacks its critics essentially as greedy polluters who spend their free time clubbing baby seals at the behest of corporate America. Their over-the-top accusations, unfortunately, are often treated seriously by their many supporters in the media. As a result, the lobby intimidates and silences many potential critics, allowing their own views to dominate the debate. Don't be fooled by their smiley-faced rhetoric about "sustainability" and "green jobs"—the environmental lobby is peddling extreme, anti-prosperity, big-government socialist policies that would spike energy prices, severely limit energy supplies, kill jobs, and depress the American economy for decades to come.

Leaders of "environmental" organizations including the Natural Resources Defense Council, Sierra Club, League of Conservation Voters, Greenpeace, and others, pursue a radical agenda that actually has little to do with the environment, and lots to do with attacking capitalism and consumer choice. America's long, noble tradition of commonsense environmental stewardship has sadly given way to extreme policies that have increased our dependence on foreign oil and raised our energy prices.

Take the environmental lobby's crusade against fossil fuels. It's no surprise that the "alternative" energy sources they favor are much more expensive than fossil fuels; that's because expensive energy is actually one of their primary goals. While most Americans welcome the economic growth, job creation, rising standard of living, and technological progress that cheap energy makes possible, radical environmentalists don't. After the 1979 energy crisis, environmental leader Steven Wilson explained the radicals' view:

> "[O]ur perception of the "energy crisis" is different from many. We feel that Americans have had too much fuel available, that less will be better. I see it as the "effects of too much energy" crisis.[5]

Thus, the environmental lobby has pursued policies for decades that have raised energy prices in an effort to stop economic growth. Here's what the outgoing leader of Greenpeace, Gerd Leipold, told the BBC:

*We will definitely have to move to a different concept of
growth. . . . The lifestyle of the rich in the world is not a sustainable model.*[6]

David Graber, who was also a U.S. government researcher and
biologist at the Fish and Wildlife Service, put it this way in 1989:

*I know social scientists who remind me that people are
part of nature, but it isn't true. Somewhere along the line—
at about a billion years ago, maybe half that—we quit the
contract and became a cancer. We have become a plague upon
ourselves and upon the Earth.*

Graber also voiced hope that mankind will be wiped out:

*It is cosmically unlikely that the developed world will
choose to end its orgy of fossil-energy consumption, and the
Third World its suicidal consumption of landscape. Until such
time as Homo sapiens should decide to rejoin nature, some of
us can only hope for the right virus to come along.*[7]

Here you see that radical environmentalism is not just anti-
growth and anti-capitalist; it is fundamentally, irredeemably
anti-human.

In response to the radicals, free market advocates argue that
responsible environmental stewardship is perfectly compatible
with, and even vital to, economic development. This view is held
by most Americans, who genuinely want to safeguard the environment. Interestingly, one American who holds this position is

Greenpeace co-founder Patrick Moore, who has become a harsh critic of the hysterical alarmism, anti-economic-growth extremism, and political gangsterism of the environmental lobby.[8]

A Doomsday Cult Goes Mainstream

Today, the environmental lobby advances its anti-growth agenda primarily by scaring people with doomsday scenarios of global warming. This tactic has been extremely successful; newspapers, television, Hollywood movies, and the Internet all bombard us with the frantic message that the planet faces certain doom if we do not stop the earth from overheating. Public schools even drill this message into our children. Instead of discussing our nation's failure to develop our own extensive natural resources, the energy debate typically focuses on how to forestall the alleged looming climate disaster.

In a nutshell, global warming theory goes like this: human emissions of greenhouse gases, particularly carbon dioxide, are heating up the Earth, threatening catastrophic floods, famines, and other apocalyptic scenarios. To avoid this horrible fate, we must drastically reduce our carbon output, which means curtailing much of our current industrial activity and our use of fossil fuels.

The science, however, never seems to cooperate with global warming theory. Carbon emissions have risen since the beginning of the Industrial Revolution in the eighteenth century, but there is no direct correlation to temperature changes. Furthermore, man-made emissions are believed to contribute about 3 percent of our atmosphere's annual carbon dioxide, with the rest being natural.[9] This underscores the unlikelihood of the connection. The U.S. government has spent over $79 billion to combat global warming, yet has failed to confirm a link between human activity and climate change.[10]

Some key scientific claims of global warming theory have been debunked in recent years. We now know that the Earth has cooled in recent years and that the temperature has fluxuated dramatically throughout history. Even one of the most prominent global warming scientists, Professor Phil Jones, former head of the Climate Research Center of East Anglia University, now admits there has been no statistically significant warming since 1995.[11]

The lack of actual warming, of course, is a major problem for global warming alarmists. So they're shifting their rhetoric from "global warming" to "climate change." The new, more flexible theory is nearly impossible to disprove, since the climate is always changing. Thus, whether we get historic snowfalls or no snow at all, whether the summer is so hot you can't go outside or colder than it's been in years, either way, alarmists can claim we're undergoing "climate change."

Whether they call it "global warming" or "climate change," environmental extremists blame man's supposed eco-sins for hurricanes, wildfires, droughts, and any other damaging natural phenomena. Some of the more ridiculous examples of climate change hysteria include allegations of: a looming crocodile gender imbalance; shrinking sheep; boy scout-killing tornados; a change in the taste of beer; the collapse of gingerbread houses in Sweden; increasing UFO sightings in the U.K.; and school children suffering from insomnia due to global warming fears. Anything can be blamed on climate change.

Contrary to the absurd alarmist propaganda, complex, natural factors largely determine our planet's climate. The Earth's history is filled with examples of warming and cooling entirely unrelated to carbon emissions. During the Medieval Warm Period (800–1300 AD), for example, temperatures averaged 2 to 4 degrees Fahrenheit warmer than today. This warming encouraged Vikings to inhabit Greenland, where they raised livestock and grew crops in a region now covered by ice.

The "Climategate" scandal of late 2009 exposed the fraudulent, politicized nature of the science behind global warming theory. The scandal unfolded when an anonymous source uploaded onto the Internet email exchanges showing Phil Jones and other prominent global warming researchers conspiring to manipulate data, suppress dissenting views, and otherwise fabricate evidence to advance their agenda. In one of many damaging e-mail exchanges, Dr. Jones said:

> *I've just completed Mike's Nature trick of adding in the real temps to each series for the last 20 years (i.e., from 1981 onwards) and from 1961 for Keith's to hide the decline.*[12]

The deceptive, unscientific methods used to promote global warming theory are clearly rooted in the age-old lust for money and power. Anyone challenging the flawed science is considered a threat to the lucrative industry that has grown around the doomsday scenario—an industry populated by current and former Washington power brokers, the environmental lobby, big business, and sundry hangers-on from the UN and other corrupt elements of the "international community."[13]

Take cap and trade, a radical leftwing proposal pushed by congressional Democrats to place a government-imposed cap on greenhouse gas emissions. Businesses could only emit carbon dioxide or other greenhouse gases if they held credits—paper notes that would initially be printed and sold by the government, and then bought and sold on a new market. The scheme potentially offers vast wealth and power for big government advocates and the environmental lobby, both of whom will gain new power over U.S. economic activity. But the big winner is big business, which could make a fortune trading carbon credits, could earn huge government subsidies by marketing useless but politically correct "green technologies," and could game cap-and-trade legislation to push its smaller competitors out of business.

Exploiting environmental issues for financial gain is certainly nothing new—just ask Al Gore, who has amassed a fortune from his green activism.[14] Meanwhile Gore, who calls for an end to carbon-based energy within ten years, owns a home that consumes twenty times more energy than that of the average American. He also wants to eliminate the internal combustion engine, but he still travels in large SUVs and private jets—all "offset" by carbon credits he charitably buys from his own company.[15]

Achieving energy independence is an urgent national priority. But our efforts are stymied by utopian environmentalists who view mankind as a plague, and by rent-seeking big businesses who willingly sacrifice our energy security for a buck. This situation has to change.

Damaging Growth and Destroying Jobs

Inexpensive, reliable energy sources created untold numbers of American jobs and built the most powerful economy in world history. Now we're told that "green jobs" are good and other jobs—

jobs that built this country—are bad. If you drive a big rig, own a farm, run cattle, or work in the timber, oil, mining, or construction industries, you're no longer viewed as a valuable contributor to our economy. Instead, you're labeled a polluter and a destroyer of the environment.

By habitually filing frivolous lawsuits, the environmental lobby exploits environmental laws and regulations to decimate entire industries and kill thousands of jobs. The cost of these lawsuits is borne by the American taxpayer. And to add insult to injury, taxpayers are forced to reimburse the environmental groups for their trouble through the Equal Access to Justice Act.

The timber industry is a good example. We produce less wood today, particularly in the west, thanks to politically motivated regulations limiting timber production. In 1965, the United States imported just under 9 million cubic meters of timber. By 2002, the number had tripled to 27.5 million, adding to our trade deficit and sending American money and jobs overseas.[16]

The issue came to a head in 1990, when the spotted owl was listed as a threatened species under the Endangered Species Act. The environmental lobby blamed the owl's plight on loggers, who lost access to millions of acres of forest throughout the Pacific Northwest; in Oregon alone, 82 percent of timber land was taken out of production, decimating many rural communities. In the last twenty-five years, timber harvests from National Forests have been reduced by 70 percent.[17]

Radical environmentalists have long sought to destroy the logging industry—a goal made possible by the Endangered Species Act. As Andy Stahl of the Sierra Club Legal Defense Fund admitted:

"And I've often thought, thank goodness the spotted owl evolved in the Northwest, or we would have had to genetically engineer it."[18]

The spotted owl became the poster child for anti-timber, anti-road access activists around the country. Thanks to these extremists, taxpayers have invested millions trying to protect the owl. Despite unprecedented restrictions on logging, however, the spotted owl population continues to decline. In fact, environmental experts now believe that logging isn't to blame for the spotted owl's decline at all. According to the U.S. Fish and Wildlife Service, the problem likely stems from competition from a more aggressive bird called the barred owl. The Fish and Wildlife Service reported in 2008:

"At this time, it appears long-term lethal control of significant numbers of barred owls should be assessed to recover the spotted owl."[19]

The Associated Press reported plainly on the government's plan:

A new recovery plan would test weeding out a number of barred owls, a program that has been tested in California. The recovery plan envisions 18 study areas, from each of which 12 to 32 animals would be removed, lured to their deaths by recorded calls and an owl decoy, then shot at close range.[20]

In short, government sharpshooters are killing barred owls to protect the endangered spotted owl—a less dominant owl species that the barred owl has pillaged to near extinction.

Sadly—but predictably—logging restrictions have not been relaxed even though experts now recognize timber harvesting did not cause the spotted owl's decline. The environmental lobby is just too powerful to give up a monumental victory like the fight

The barred owl (left) is taking over the spotted owl's (right) habitat. A 2008 government report recommends killing barred owls to assist in the spotted owl's recovery. (Photos by David Arbour, Washington Department of Fish and Wildlife [left]; U.S. Geological Survey [right])

over the spotted owl just because they were spectacularly wrong on the facts.

The Big Oil Conspiracy

If you follow the news, you've no doubt heard many attacks by the environmental lobby on "big oil," one of the lobby's favorite targets. In order to make their case, however, the lobby misrepresents the basic facts about our oil industry.

It's true that the bulk of oil consumed in the United States is refined and marketed by so-called "big oil"—ExxonMobil, Chevron, Shell, BP, and other independent, American or European oil companies. Most of the oil, however, is imported from a number of foreign sources. Only 6 percent of global crude oil supplies is controlled by independent companies.[21]

The remaining oil, representing 94 percent of global resources, is either directly or indirectly controlled by foreign governments. These governments conspire to manipulate global supplies in order to keep prices high. Additionally, alliances between oil producers have created a market dominated by the Organization of Petroleum Exporting Countries (OPEC), a cartel whose members include Venezuela, Iran, Saudi Arabia, Nigeria, Libya, Iraq, and six other countries. OPEC is an expert at one thing: fixing world oil prices. And OPEC does what's in the best interests of OPEC. Because of our unnecessary dependence on foreign oil, we are picking up the tab.

Fossil Fuel Wars

In order to counter the environmental lobby's slanders, private oil companies are spending tens of millions of dollars on deceptive advertising to promote their "green credentials." BP's makeover from British Petroleum to Beyond Petroleum, for example, was part of a massive public relations campaign to paint the oil company green. And BP is not alone; for instance, natural gas companies are attacking other fossil fuels as "dirty."

Oil companies engage in these attacks as a way to profit from global warming hysteria. But this rhetoric undermines sensible energy policy and misleads the public while empowering the environmental lobby. Giving in to extortion by radical environmentalists, oil firms are perpetuating the myth that we can live on just solar and wind power. As President Ronald Reagan once said:

To sit back hoping that someday, some way, someone will make things right is to go on feeding the crocodile, hoping he will eat you last—but eat you he will.

Big oil is feeding the crocodile. Shell, BP, and ConocoPhillips even joined the U.S. Climate Action Partnership, an extremist organization advocating federal laws limiting carbon emissions. The companies may be trying to limit the scope of these proposed laws, but by joining the climate change charade, they legitimized it. Perhaps realizing this, in early 2010 BP and ConocoPhillips abruptly withdrew from the group, which still retains numerous other big energy and finance companies.[22] The point is this: instead of educating Americans on the facts of our energy consumption and long-term needs, many fossil fuel companies and utilities are helping the environmental lobby create a future of high prices and energy shortages in the United States.

The BRIC Challenge

As so many of our own energy reserves remain off-limits, BRIC countries (Brazil, Russia, India, and China) have assumed the lead role in global energy. America once dominated the oil market, consuming the bulk of global energy resources and facing only limited competition from other developed nations. But it's different today. Based on current trends, world energy demand will increase 50 percent or more in twenty years. India and China could account for nearly half this increase.

The United States is quickly falling behind our global competitors in energy development. In the short-term, the BRICs are extensively exploring and developing fossil fuels, including natural gas, coal, and oil, to promote robust economic growth. Long-term, they are investing in nuclear power, coal-to-liquid technology, and large-scale hydroelectric facilities. A quick look at each BRIC country shows the challenges we face from our current and future competitors.

Brazil

Brazil is rapidly becoming a major producer and consumer of energy. With the fifth largest population in the world (approaching 200 million), diverse and rich geography, and policies that encourage energy exploration, Brazil is growing fast, as is its standard of living.

Brazil is often noted for its aggressive promotion of ethanol use, but the key to its energy riches has really been hydropower and oil. Until very recently, Brazil had few proven oil reserves, relying on the production and use of sugar cane ethanol instead. In the last decade, however, the country used U.S. technology to locate enormous supplies of offshore oil that could make Brazil one of the world's largest oil producers. Tens of billions of dollars have now been committed to developing Brazil's offshore energy resources, including investment from Chinese oil companies. Notably, the U.S. Export-Import bank has given loans to U.S. companies to assist Brazil's offshore oil development.[23] In other words, the U.S. government is hostile to offshore energy development in the United States, but perversely, it's happy to help turn Brazil into an energy powerhouse, and in turn, an economic competitor.

Russia

Although the true extent of Russia's energy supplies is unclear, we know Russia's projected energy resources are second only to the United States. In addition to being the world's largest producer of natural gas, it vies with Saudi Arabia as the world's largest oil producer, and it's also a major coal producer. Much of its energy production is exported to its European neighbors, increasing Russia's influence throughout the continent. The huge revenues from its energy exports go to help diversify Russia's economy, to finance further energy development, and to create "stabilization funds" that can be tapped during economic crises, among other uses.

India

With more than a billion people, India has the world's second largest population, and is expected to surpass China's population in the next decade. Experiencing near double digit economic growth, the country is struggling to develop reliable and affordable energy resources for its growing middle class. India was already the world's fourth largest oil consumer,[24] and Indian officials estimate that national energy consumption will quadruple over the next twenty-five years.

In response, India has developed an aggressive nuclear power program. Although the country is investing in alternative and renewable energy, the Indian government is also committed to developing vast domestic fossil fuel resources. This includes its recent completion of the world's largest oil refinery complex, which will partially be used to meet growing U.S. demand due to our own failure to develop new refineries. Soon, we will be importing not only foreign oil, but larger amounts of refined energy products.

China

In sharp contrast to the United States, which has virtually halted oil and gas exploration on federal lands, China is aggressively exploring both domestic and foreign energy resources, especially fossil fuels. Additionally, China operates eleven nuclear power plants today, it has twenty more on the horizon, more than a hundred in long-term development, and the country is building the world's largest hydroelectric facility, the Three Gorges Dam.

China's direct foreign investment in international energy projects include interests in Venezuela, Sudan, West Africa, Iran, Saudi Arabia, Russia, Kazakhstan, and Canada. In the Gulf of Mexico, just forty-five miles from the U.S. coastline, China is working with Cuba to develop off-shore oil and gas resources in areas adjacent to those our own government has prevented American oil companies from drilling.[25] China is also working to exploit existing oil leases in the Gulf, including those in American territory.[26]

The Threat

Our dependence on foreign oil leaves us vulnerable to disruptions in oil supplies and even to economic sabotage. This happened before, when we faced an Arab oil embargo because of our support for Israel during the Yom Kippur War in October 1973. At the time we only imported 36 percent of our oil, compared to some 60 percent now.[27] The long gas lines back then were bad enough (at least I imagine they were—I was in a car seat at the time), but imagine what draconian restrictions we'd have to adopt if we faced another embargo today.

In some ways, our oil supply is even more volatile today than it was in the 1970s. Back then, at least the Arabs who enacted the embargo were rational actors pursuing a specific goal: to reduce our support for Israel. (Thankfully, it didn't work.) Today, some of our key suppliers are unbalanced individuals who may be clinically insane. These include Venezuela's dictator Hugo Chavez, who repeatedly referred to former President George W. Bush as the devil. Chavez, who has vowed to "bury the United States," could do serious harm to global energy markets by using oil as a weapon. He's already shown that he holds little respect for international norms, for example, by ordering his army in 2007 to seize oil production infrastructure that was built and operated by American and European energy companies.

Venezuela is allied with Iran, a regime filled with Islamic fanatics and led by the crackpot ayatollah Ali Khamenei and his unhinged lackey, Mahmoud Ahmadinejad. Their goals include destroying Israel, gaining nuclear weapons, and exporting their twisted brand of Islamic fundamentalism around the world. A leading oil producer, Iran is extremely influential on the international oil market. As a rogue nation, Iran presents a real threat through its ability to disrupt the global energy market.

In addition to outright hostility from oil producers, we face the constant risk of regional instability. Independent oil companies in Nigeria such as Royal Dutch Shell operate in the river delta region, where gangsters, ethnic militias, and armed local residents have all violently clashed over oil revenues. These conflicts have triggered attacks on oil facilities, resulting in the destruction of entire villages and the mass murder of innocent people. And America imports roughly half of Nigeria's oil, making Nigeria one of our most important oil suppliers.

The bottom line is that we are dangerously dependent on a volatile supply of foreign oil. This entire situation is unnecessary because the United States has the natural resources and access to

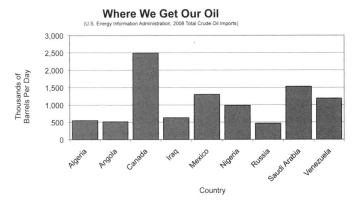

Where We Get Our Oil
(U.S. Energy Information Administration, 2008 Total Crude Oil Imports)

The United States is forced to compete for oil on the international market where regional instability creates significant price volatility. (U.S. Energy Information Administration, U.S. Imports by Country of Origin, 6/29/2009)

renewable energy to become energy secure—it's just that our government won't let us develop them. As our dependence on foreign oil continues to rise, the risk of shortages increases and our trade deficit grows. In any given year, half our trade deficit—money paid to foreign governments—is used to pay for foreign oil. This money should have stayed in the pockets of American families, including yours and mine.

SOLUTION

Congress must address the short-term needs and long-term prospects of America's energy demand. Recognizing the importance of these two goals, I introduced legislation called "A Roadmap for America's Energy Future" that would lead to the creation of millions of American jobs and create a stable supply of domestically produced energy. And since it would also set us on a path toward real carbon reductions worldwide, even global warming alarmists can get behind the plan. What follows is an outline of the plan's main components.

Oil and Gas

The Energy Roadmap would allow our nation to develop a minimum of 136 billion barrels of oil from the Arctic National Wildlife Refuge (ANWR) and the Outer Continental Shelf. Tapping these abundant resources would eliminate our dependence on Middle Eastern oil and lower energy prices. Despite what you may hear in the media, we can reduce oil and gas prices by drilling in our own country.

Kickstarting Alaskan drilling is particularly important. The construction of the Alaskan pipeline began in 1975 to tap the oil reserves in Alaska's North Slope. With a capacity of 2 million barrels of oil per day, it is now the most important U.S. pipeline, accounting for around 18 percent of all U.S. oil production. But it only pumps one-third of its capacity, or 770,000 barrels per day, because the environmental lobby has blocked further oil exploration along Alaska's North Slope. By 2020, it could reach the minimum amount of oil needed to keep it operational. Meanwhile, proposals to build a separate pipeline to transport Alaska's abundant natural gas supply to mainland America are stalled in the federal bureaucracy.

Radical environmentalists often frame their opposition to Alaskan oil and gas drilling as a defense of the caribou. They imply these are rare, endangered, delicate creatures, when in fact the caribou are so robust in Alaska that they outnumber humans—686,293 people versus 900,000-plus caribou. Caribou are simply a member of the deer family and are numerous throughout the world. As for the harm that pipelines and drilling supposedly do to the caribou, the Alaska Department of Fish and Game reports,

> *Although there was some displacement of caribou calving in the Prudhoe Bay oilfield, in general, caribou have not been adversely affected by human activities in Alaska.*[28]

In fact, in the North Slope area, the caribou have flourished. The Central Arctic Herd increased from an estimated 3,000 in the early 1970s to 32,000 in 2002 and 67,000 in 2008.[29]

One little-known fact is that Alaska loses tens of thousands of caribou a year through hunting, an activity proudly promoted by the Alaska Department of Fish and Game, which states:

> *Alaska hunters shoot about 22,000 caribou each year for food. A few thousand other hunters, primarily from the lower 48 states, Europe, and Mexico, travel to Alaska to experience caribou hunting each fall. These hunters contribute significant-ly to the economy of the state, particularly in rural areas.*[30]

News of the resiliency of Alaska's caribou has begun filtering into the debate, meaning the environmental lobby had to recruit another lovable creature into its anti-drilling campaign. Enter the polar bear, the newest, cutest animal supposedly driven by mankind to the brink of extinction. Unsurprisingly, big business has taken up the campaign. Coca Cola, which depicts huggable polar bears in its Christmas-time advertising, reports in its Polar Bear Support Fund:

> *For many of us, the polar bear symbolizes the joy of coming together for the holidays. The polar bear has also become a symbol for global climate change, as the disappearance of its arctic habitat hinders reproduction and overall well-being.*[31]

Is the polar bear really threatened? No. In fact, the polar bear population has grown from around 5,000 fifty years ago to 25,000 today.[32] Nevertheless, in October 2009 the Department of the Interior designated more than 200,000 square miles of land, sea, and ice along Alaska's Northern Slope as critical habitat to protect the bear. This action was taken at the behest of the environmental lobby, which cites global warming and melting arctic ice as a threat to the polar bear's survival.

Notably, the critical habitat designation does not provide evidence of an existing threat to the species. Changing arctic ice conditions pre-date human existence and have not resulted in a collapse of the species. And while there was a significant retreat of polar ice in the 1990s, that trend has since reversed.

The false alarm over polar bears has damaged American energy development and placed our nation at significant risk. We have put many of our own abundant oil and gas reserves off-limits as we import more and more foreign oil. Meanwhile, even overseas competitors like China are drilling around the continental United States. Near ANWR, Canada is exploring offshore oil resources. And other competitors, most notably Russia, have staked major claims over arctic energy reserves. As the environmental lobby ties up every new energy project in years of litigation, foreign governments are setting up projects on our borders to take North American energy reserves right out from under us.

We also need to fully open the Outer Continental Shelf, the areas off our east and west coasts that potentially hold enormous reserves of oil and natural gas. (We're not sure how many energy resources are there, because for decades we've *banned ourselves* from exploring it.) Recently, the Obama administration trumpeted its decision to open limited areas off the southern east coast, Alaska, and the Gulf of Mexico to oil drilling. Far from opening new areas, however, what Obama actually did was to *ban* drilling from most of our coasts. The areas "opened" by Obama, in fact, had been open since congressional and presidential drilling bans were lifted in 2008. Obama's policy effectively blocks drilling from the entire Pacific coast, which has more oil than all the newly opened areas combined.[33] House Speaker Nancy Pelosi clarified the president's intent. "The president was actually narrowing drilling," she said, "It isn't as if the president expanded drilling."[34]

Even the limited new drilling allowed by Obama is unlikely to proceed, since the president suspended steps toward offshore drilling expansion following the Deepwater Horizon oil spill in the Gulf of Mexico. Congress will now be locked up in hearings and investigations indefinitely. Although the oil spill was a terrible accident with severe environmental repercussions, it should not be used as an excuse to ban new drilling. There's no avoiding the fact that we need more oil. If we don't drill, we'll just become ever more reliant on foreign oil—and importing oil on tankers actually carries more environmental risks than offshore drilling.[35] Limiting our own drilling while other countries continue theirs will not make the environment any safer. The right move is to use the accident as an opportunity to improve drilling safety, not to exploit it to completely shut down new drilling.

Moreover, by banning drilling off California, the administration is sacrificing billions of dollars in potential tax revenue desperately needed by both California and the federal government. As energy consultant Michael Lynch wrote in the *New York Times*:

> This area, especially off Southern California, has an estimated 7.5 billion to 14 billion barrels of oil and 13 trillion to 24 trillion cubic feet of natural gas. It could probably generate as much revenue as the other newly released areas combined; the oil, not having to be piped from northern Alaska, would be cheaper to harvest. While California drilling is one of the third rails of American politics, the federal government forgoing at least $20 billion a year in taxes seems unwise.[36]

The president's new policy also kept ANWR closed, and even cancelled planned lease sales in Bristol Bay, one of Alaska's most promising areas for oil development. What's more, it's unclear whether any drilling will ultimately be allowed in the areas opened in 2008, since oil companies will have to wait through years of impact studies and public meetings before any leases could be offered. After all that, if a lease were offered, as sure as the sun shines the environmental lobby will file frivolous legal challenges to delay drilling for years longer.

Nuclear

Modern nuclear energy exists largely thanks to President Eisenhower, who promoted civilian nuclear power through a program known as Atoms for Peace. Frustrated with the slow development of private-sector nuclear energy, Eisenhower tapped Admiral Hyman Rickover (who in 1955 had successfully deployed the first nuclear-powered naval vessel, the *Nautilus*) to build the first civilian nuclear plant. The reactor, located in Shippingport, Pennsylvania, began operating in 1957, initially producing sixty megawatts of energy. Later, it was upgraded to produce 100 megawatts.

The USS *Nautilus*, the world's first nuclear powered vessel (Photo by U.S. Navy)

Eisenhower intended the Shippingport plant to serve as a model for future civilian nuclear facilities. As such, the government declassified documents detailing the plant's construction and operation. These provided the basis for the groundbreaking progress in nuclear power achieved by mid-twentieth-century scientists and engineers who brought America a reliable, clean, and inexpensive source of energy.[37]

Despite these advantages, however, nuclear power only supplies 8.6 percent of our total energy today, and just 20 percent of our electricity. Although many claim nuclear power is stymied by safety concerns, nuclear energy is entirely safe. In the more than fifty years that civilian nuclear plants have operated in the United States, there has not been a single fatal reactor failure. But nuclear power is often *perceived* as being unsafe. Why? Because anti-nuclear activists have deceitfully spread this idea for at least three decades.

Exhibit A in the anti-nuclear propaganda campaign is the accident at the Three Mile Island nuclear plant located near Harrisburg, Pennsylvania. On March 28, 1979, equipment malfunctions, design problems, and worker error resulted in a partial meltdown of one of the reactor cores. The meltdown was significant, but it did not breach the containment system, cause any injuries, or release a significant amount of radioactive material. The surrounding community registered no measurable increase in radiation during or after the event.[38]

However, the timing of the incident couldn't have been worse. On March 16, 1979, *The China Syndrome* opened in theatres around the country. The Hollywood production depicted a near-catastrophic accident at a nuclear reactor and the subsequent cover-up by company officials. Hollywood icon and far-left activist Jane Fonda played a righteous character fighting to expose the danger of a possible core meltdown. That danger, referred to as the China Syndrome, wildly suggests that molten material from an American nuclear reactor can escape containment and melt through the earth's crust, all the way to China.

Following the Three Mile Island accident, anti-nuclear energy activists gained national attention. This rally was held at the state capitol in Harrisburg, Pennsylvania, on April 4, 1979. (Photo courtesy of National Archives and Records Administration)

This scenario was a little different from what happened at Three Mile Island, where the molten material only penetrated 5/8 of an inch of the containment system. Dr. Theodore Rockwell, who served under Admiral Rickover, is a nuclear energy pioneer and was Technical Director on the *Nautilus* project. He was present at the start of the nation's first nuclear reactor and was part of the Three Mile Island damage assessment team. Speaking to me of the meltdown, Rockwell invoked an ancient Chinese proverb:

"A journey of a thousand miles must begin with a single step."

Five-eights of an inch, Rockwell joked, doesn't even qualify as a single step.

While *The China Syndrome* made for an entertaining movie, its catastrophic premise was pure fiction. Nevertheless, environmental extremists exploited the story to spread unjustified fears about nuclear power. The safe containment of the accident at Three Mile Island actually should have bolstered our confidence. Today, the facility continues to produce 786 megawatts of electricity.

Unfortunately, the demonizing of nuclear power has been so effective that no new nuclear facility has been built in the United States in thirty years. We have abandoned safe, clean, and inexpensive nuclear energy for high-cost, low-return energy sources such as solar and wind power. Although these kinds of renewable energy sources will be important components of a more diverse energy portfolio, they cannot provide the base-load power needed by our growing economy. To replace a single nuclear reactor would require 3.3 million solar panels, assuming it doesn't get foggy or cloudy outside. That's why long-term energy reform must include greater use of advanced nuclear technology.

In France, 80 percent of electricity comes from nuclear power. This should be our goal. In order to achieve it, the Energy Roadmap calls for granting 200 nuclear permits. President Obama took a comically insufficient step in this direction when he approved loan guarantees to build two new reactors at an existing nuclear plant. While I applaud the president for approving 1 percent of the number of new reactors we need, there is a lot more work to be done. Since Obama often pays lip service to nuclear power, Congress should help him along by requiring the president to issue permits.

Coal and Oil Shale

The United States has at least a 250-year supply of affordable coal. Modern coal technologies permit coal gasification, as well as the conversion of coal into a liquid form. These refinements make it easier for coal to serve as a substitute for foreign oil and can significantly reduce environmental concerns. This process is similar to that used to extract oil from shale deposits, which is another potential major source of fuel. It is estimated our shale deposits in the Green River Formation in Wyoming, Utah, and Colorado have three times as much oil as all of Saudi Arabia,[39] though the environmental lobby has successfully put most of this huge supply off-limits.

New forms of coal energy have enormous potential, but they require major investments in new technology. Additionally, Congress will have to allow access to big coal deposits that are now off-limits. The Energy Roadmap makes it possible for the United States to utilize fully this abundant resource. Furthermore, it will allow the military to replace oil with liquid coal. This will reduce our nation's consumption of oil, helping to ease market pressure while spurring the large-scale production of liquid coal.

Energy Diversity

By allowing U.S. energy developers to access domestic oil and gas, the policies in the Energy Roadmap will raise tens of billions of dollars from royalties and leases. The Departments of Energy and Interior estimate total federal revenues could reach an astounding $60 trillion from this kind of energy development. These dollars would be deposited into an energy independence trust fund that would fund clean, renewable, and other alternative energy forms. Thus, if Congress passed the Energy Roadmap, it would be the largest investment in clean, renewable energy in the history of the planet.

These policies would also create hundreds of thousands of American jobs—jobs lost today due to our dependence on foreign oil. As previously mentioned, this clean, abundant energy would also set us on a path toward real carbon reductions worldwide, a prospect sure to warm the hearts of global warming alarmists everywhere. These jobs are what I call "real green jobs," as opposed to the phantom green jobs that we're told the government is creating, but which really don't exist.

In sum, the Energy Roadmap will bring our nation affordable energy and a cleaner environment—two goals that are not mutually exclusive.

Radical Environmentalism Is Communism

Green radicals abandoned the principles of a clean, healthy environment many years ago. Today, they are pursuing a radical agenda that seeks to replace capitalism with a Marxist utopia. The views of this powerful minority are against human progress and can only be described as regressive. I received a lot of flack from the media for saying the following at a summer 2009 speech before tea party activists in Sacramento, California:

"Today's radical environmentalist is yesterday's Communist."

The California paper the *Fresno Bee* commented:

> *So now the congressman who doesn't believe in protecting our natural resources is calling people communists for wanting their children to breathe clean air.*

What the editorialists refused to accept or preferred not to report is that the environmental lobby indeed comprises followers of neo-Marxist, socialist, Maoist, or Communist ideals. They use environmental pieties to cover an extremist agenda that seeks the redistribution of wealth and the abolition of free markets in favor of centralized economic control. Czech Republic president Vaclav Klaus can speak with some authority on this, having suffered for years under a bona fide Communist regime. And when it comes to the effect of global warming laws, he sees some disturbing similarities:

> *We'll be the victims of irrational ideology. They [global warming alarmists] will try to dictate to us how to live, what to do, how to behave. . . . What to eat, travel, and what my children should have. This is something that we who lived in the communist era for most of our lives—we still feel very strongly about.*[40]

We Americans owe our national success to our commitment to capitalism, entrepreneurship, and cultivation of a cheap, abundant energy supply. To continue this unparalleled economic achievement, the United States must pursue an all-of-the-above energy plan with a heavy focus on clean nuclear power, while using our own fossil fuels to build a bridge to the next generation of energy. The Energy Roadmap outlines the way to this bright future of abundance and prosperity.

CHAPTER FOUR

THE BIG THREE

*"For God's sake don't let dead cats
stand on your porch."*
—President Lyndon Johnson

BACKGROUND

WHEN I REFER TO THE BIG THREE IN GOVERNMENT, I AM NOT
talking about American automakers—even though taxpayers now
own one of them. I am referring to the big three federal entitlement programs, Social Security, Medicaid, and Medicare.

Social Security is the federal program that provides retirement
benefits from the age of sixty-seven or reduced benefits from the
age of sixty-two. The program is funded by payroll taxes, which
are direct deductions from the paychecks of working Americans.
Employers are mandated to collect this tax, which is shared
equally by the employer and the employee. An individual's right
to Social Security benefits is in a sense "earned," but benefits are

not directly measured by the amount of payments made into the system; Congress has determined the levels of benefits under the Social Security Act, as well as the conditions upon which they may be paid.

Medicaid is the federal program that provides health insurance to low-income Americans. It is administered by state governments but is subject to federal mandates. As a result, Medicaid has taken many forms across the United States, with funding traditionally balanced between federal and state contributions. In recent years Congress has increased federal payments, placing larger burdens on the federal budget.

Medicare is the federal program that provides health insurance to all Americans aged sixty-five and older. It is financed partly by payroll taxes. Congress has significantly expanded the program since its creation in 1965, when it was simply a hospital benefit. Today, Medicare spending includes inpatient hospital care, outpatient care, physician services, and prescription drug coverage, among other benefits. Although many people believe payroll taxes pay for Medicare benefits, general tax dollars now account for 39 percent of overall program spending.[1]

PROBLEM

Early one morning in late 2009, I was walking down the halls of Congress and ran into my friend, Congressman Paul Ryan of Wisconsin. Earlier in the year, Paul and I worked with Senators Tom Coburn (a physician) of Oklahoma and Richard Burr of North Carolina on a healthcare bill that provided universal coverage and that made solvent one of our unfunded entitlement programs, Medicaid.

Paul and I had worked tirelessly with other Republicans to unite Congress around a healthcare bill. Our plan, the Patients' Choice Act, was introduced in Congress long before any of the Democratic proposals emerged. But the Democrats had no interest in bipartisan, practical, commonsense reform, preferring an extreme course of setting America on a path to Canadian-style or British-style government-run healthcare. Having frequently discussed the problem of our unfunded liabilities in Medicaid, Medicare, and Social Security, we often shared our frustration that no one seemed to notice the mountain of debt we are leaving to future generations. That morning Paul told me,

"The bottom line is, no one wants to walk through the fire."

Paul was right. Politicians don't want to deal with a problem, any problem, if they can push it off into the future. The liabilities faced by the Big Three are a perfect example—no one wants to address the debt we acknowledge, the $13 trillion in federal debt, let alone the debt we ignore, the $67 trillion in unfunded liabilities associated with entitlement programs.

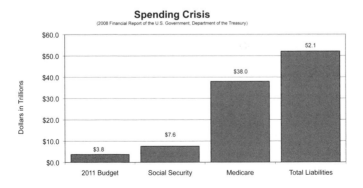

(2008 U.S. Financial Statement, Department of the Treasury)

The Democratic healthcare bill will only make things worse. Disguised by accounting tricks as a deficit reducing measure, the bill creates a huge new entitlement at a time when our existing entitlements are already driving us toward national bankruptcy.

Social Security

The Social Security Trustees' report has explained to Congress for years that the program is on an unsustainable path. Congress has occasionally tinkered with the program to buy time, for example, by raising the retirement age. But this only delays the inevitable financial meltdown.

Consistently blocking efforts to protect the program's long-term viability, congressional Democrats shamelessly distort reform proposals in order to scare elderly voters. They refuse to address core challenges that will bankrupt the program, including the fact that it's dependent on a high worker-to-retiree ratio, and it earns lower returns than even the safest private retirement plans. Perhaps most vexing, Social Security has no mechanism to actually save the money it receives in "trust" for workers. Instead of investing the funds like private firms, Social Security buys Treasury bonds that create public debt. In other words, the only way for the program to save money is to create government debt.

A lot has changed over the years to make Social Security unsustainable. For example, when the Social Security program was created in 1935, the average working man could expect to live to the age of sixty-three. Since the retirement age was initially set at sixty-five, most Americans didn't live long enough to receive any benefits in the early years of the program. Since then, the average life expectancy has increased to nearly eighty, but Congress has only pushed back the retirement age by two years.

Another problematic trend affects Social Security's funding mechanism; in 1935, 42 workers paid Social Security taxes for every retired American. By 1950 this number had dropped to 16, and in 2010 it is just 3.3. By 2030, 2.2 workers will be paying into the system for each retiree, meaning benefits will exceed the program's income from payroll taxes beginning as early as 2017.[2]

Although the Social Security Trust Fund has positive balances today (including interest income), these funds are projected to be exhausted by 2039.[3] Furthermore, in order to use these "surplus" balances, which are held in the form of Treasury Notes (bonds), we have to spend general fund tax dollars. In other words, we have to buy back the bonds. There are only two ways to do that: by raising taxes or cutting spending.

The bottom line is that the federal government's only mechanism for saving is to create internal debt by purchasing its own bonds—an accounting gimmick that would put a corporate executive behind bars. No other American institution, public or private, saves in this manner—and for good reason. *The savings do not actually exist.* They are simply a promise dependent on increased future tax collections.

Mind you, members of Congress and government employees can expect to earn far more retirement savings than the average American. This is because they have an exclusive program of personal accounts, known as the Thrift Savings Plan, that is funded through contributions from both the government and the employee. But unlike Social Security, the accounts are controlled by the employee, not the government. Individuals can invest in stock and bond funds set up by regulators—safe investment options that offer significantly better long-term benefits than Social Security. It's quite remarkable that for their own retirement, politicians and government employees need to buttress their Social Security with what you might call a "private option."

Recognizing the injustice of the current Social Security system and its looming collapse, President George W. Bush called on Congress to enact reforms. Congressional Democrats overwhelmingly opposed him, even launching a national campaign that demonized Republicans for wanting to "privatize" Social Security.

In 2005, the Ways and Means Committee held a hearing on Social Security reform featuring testimony from expert witnesses.[4] As the committee's newest member, I asked the last questions. I tried to impress upon everyone the fact that Democrats were playing political games instead of offering real reform proposals. Here is my exchange with the panel:

> *Mr. NUNES.* Did you hear any of the Democrats today offer a plan to save Social Security, Mr. Lindsey?
> *Mr. LAWRENCE LINDSEY.* No.
> *Mr. NUNES.* Mr. Pozen, did you—
> *Mr. ROBERT POZEN.* I heard a witness say the Orzag-Diamond plan, but I haven't yet heard any Congressperson say they were willing to propose that package of several tax increases and benefit constraints. It is an honest plan, but I haven't heard a politician adopt it yet.
> *Mr. NUNES.* Mr. Schieber?
> *Mr. SYLVESTER SCHIEBER.* No.
> *Mr. NUNES.* Dr. Steuerle?
> *Mr. EUGENE STEUERLE.* Pass.

[Laughter.]

Mr. NUNES. Mr. Apfel?

Mr. KENNETH APFEL. You asked whether elected officials have proposed plans?

Mr. NUNES. Any today during this hearing where we have been discussing what to do about the future of Social Security.

Mr. KENNETH APFEL. I have not heard any plans that did not increase borrowing dramatically to pay for Social Security to solve the long-term solvency problem.

Mr. NUNES. Have you heard plans, at least proposed, by the Republican side of the aisle?

Mr. KENNETH APFEL. That entailed drastic levels of new borrowing that I think put Social Security benefits at risk.

Mr. NUNES. That is fair enough that you have your points on the legislation, but at least there have been plans that have been offered for discussion, which I think is important to have all of you here to analyze that, these plans, and add to the discussion, and I want to thank all of you for dedicating a large portion of your life to trying to solve these problems that we face with Social Security. I appreciate your opinion that there are problems with the plans on this side of the aisle. Well, it is better than having no plan, in my opinion. Dr. Hunter?

Mr. LAWRENCE HUNTER. I did not hear any plans from the other side of the aisle today, but I will tell you, and the good news is that, especially before this last Presidential election, I spent many hours on Capitol Hill talking to Democrats on this side and on the other side of the Capitol, and I will tell you that there are many who are very interested in personal accounts, and that is the reason I started off this morning by saying—it seems like a long time ago now—that unfortunately, the political climate may not be right to do it all, right now. That is the reason I encourage the Committee to do what I think is perhaps possible, and with the Chairman's [William M. Thomas (CA)] leadership this may actually happen, because everyone, everyone in the country realizes it is wrong to spend the surplus, and a good number of your colleagues on both sides of the aisle recognize that the best thing to do with those surpluses is to invest them. We can have an interesting debate on how they should be invested, but I think we have a real opportunity here, and you may not get very many Democrats right now, but I have confidence this is a long process and this is a beginning, and I commend the Chairman for holding this hearing.

Mr. NUNES. Thank you. Dr. Furman?

Mr. JASON FURMAN. It has been a long hearing, and I may have missed it, but I actually didn't hear anyone on the Republican side, on this side, embrace any specific steps to improve solvency in terms of reducing benefits or raising revenues. If you want to transfer general fund revenue to Social Security, you can extend solvency, but I didn't hear any specific steps. In fact—

Mr. NUNES. You heard specific plans laid on the table?

Mr. JASON FURMAN. The one specific step I heard from anyone here today that would improve our long-run fiscal outlook was Mr. Pomeroy and the estate tax proposal. I don't think I heard anything else that would, but you can correct me if I am wrong, if anyone—now, I have heard a lot of things from the panel, Bob Pozen's ideas, what a lot of other people have. I didn't hear anyone up there embracing them. I only heard about ideas that would cost money, not save money.

Mr. NUNES. Thank you, Dr. Furman. Mr. Tanner?

Mr. MICHAEL TANNER. Yes. I heard several proposals on the Republican side. The proposal by Representative Johnson, by Mr. Ryan, by Mr. Shaw, all of them scored by the Social Security actuaries as restoring Social Security to permanent sustainable solvency. From the Democratic side, I did not hear any proposals at all for restoring solvency or fixing any of the other problems within Social Security, which is really a shame, because this used to be a very bipartisan issue. Members like your former colleague, Charlie Stenholm, or Members from the other body like Senator Robb, Senator Kerry, Senator Moynihan—all who supported individual accounts at one time or another and were very willing to take up Social Security reform in a bipartisan manner—are gone and it seems to be now simply a matter of misinformation and very partisan debate on that side of the aisle and it is a shame. I say this as someone who is not a Republican, that I am very disappointed.

Mr. NUNES. Thank you, Mr. Tanner. This being my
first day on the Committee, Mr. Chairman, I am a little
bit disappointed to hear none of my colleagues on the
Democrat side of the aisle offer any alternatives. I hope
that the next hearing when I get to attend a full
Committee hearing that we will actually have some ideas
by the Democrats that have been laid out on the table.
Until then, unfortunately, the Republicans have to
debate amongst ourselves. We have many different ideas,
and we are using many of your ideas and many of the
proposals that have been put upon the table. It sure
would be nice to have at least some input from the
Democrat side of the aisle. With that, Mr. Chairman,
thank you for the welcome to the Committee.

Obviously, Democratic lawmakers weren't taking reform seriously.
They were only interested in exploiting the issue for political gain,
and they even heckled President Bush over it during his 2005
State of the Union address. Unfortunately, their demagoguery was
pretty successful, forcing Republicans to retreat from the issue in
2006. Other issues took center stage—the Iraq war, Hurricane
Katrina, even Vice President Cheney's hunting accident—and
Congress once again ignored this impending crisis.

Medicaid

Medicaid is becoming the American version of socialized
medicine. Because state and federal government control and
finance the program, political considerations drive decision making instead of best medical practices or, most important, the needs

of patients. Rationing in Medicaid is a serious problem; payments to doctors are so low that in many cases they're below the cost of delivering services. This drives a lot of doctors out of Medicaid, denying the best available care to vulnerable groups. In some states, less than a third of doctors will see Medicaid patients, and many communities don't have a single doctor who will.

Medicaid was created as part of President Lyndon Johnson's Great Society initiative in 1965. This period was a high water mark for big government activists, who successfully transferred control over many aspects of the economy from individual states to Washington bureaucrats. Over the years, Medicaid has vastly expanded from its origins as a safety-net healthcare program for low-income Americans. In some states, coverage is now afforded to people with incomes as high as 300 percent above the poverty level.[5]

After blocking for years any effort to improve Medicaid, in 2010 the Democrats passed the healthcare reform bill. This will add around 16 million more Americans to a failing program that the federal government and the states already cannot afford. Although the federal government will at first pick up the tab for these new patients, the states will have to pay for the program's administrative costs, and over time they will have to help cover the patients' benefits as well.

This explains why the most widely reviled bribes the Democrats offered senators to get the healthcare bill passed—Ben Nelson's "Cornhusker Kickback" and Mary Landrieu's "Louisiana Purchase"—increased federal funding for Medicaid in Nebraska and Louisiana, respectively. Even without having to cover millions of new Medicaid patients, many states are desperate to find a way to pay for the program. The healthcare bill's expansion of Medicaid will force many cash-strapped states either to raise taxes, cut other programs, reduce Medicaid benefits, or reduce Medicaid's reimbursement rates for doctors.[6] Although Democrats claim the bill will encourage more doctors to treat Medicaid patients by raising their reimbursement rate, that's highly unlikely, since this clause only lasts two years.

Medicaid is a program whose main function, increasingly, is to provide states with a means to extort federal tax dollars. There are much better ways to increase healthcare access than dumping millions more Americans into this dysfunctional, unsustainable program.

Medicare

Also created as part of President Johnson's Great Society, Medicare initially served only as a hospital benefit. Eligibility was set at sixty-five years of age, which helped keep costs down during the program's early years.[7] However, life expectancy has risen from sixty-nine to seventy-seven since the first beneficiary became eligible, adding considerably to the cost.[8]

As life expectancy has risen, so too has Medicare's coverage—the program now covers all aspects of modern healthcare. Medicare Part A, the hospital portion of the program, is funded by dedicated payroll taxes. When you see withholding in your paycheck for Medicare, you are paying for hospital benefits that seniors are receiving today. However, expansions in coverage have been funded through general tax revenues. These expansions range from the creation of Medicare Part B in 1983, which covers outpatient doctors' visits, to Medicare Part D in 2003, which provides prescription drug coverage.

Medicare's financial trouble partly stems from Congress expanding coverage without determining how to pay for it. It is also because, much like Social Security, Medicare depends on a large workforce to support it. As the taxpaying workforce declines and the senior population grows, Medicare moves closer to insolvency.

Additionally, evolving medical practices, longer life expectancy, and the prevalence of treatable but chronic medical conditions in our country have made the program impossibly expensive. The hospital insurance trust fund, Medicare Part A, will be fully depleted in 2017.[9] As is the case with Social Security, payroll taxes will have to be raised to cover the Medicare hospital benefit, and we'd need an even larger general tax increase to adequately fund outpatient visits and other basic medical coverage that is now covered by general tax revenue.

In short, having amassed long-term liabilities of $38 trillion, Medicare is eating up the federal budget and will comprise 35 percent of federal spending by 2040.[10] Simply cutting $500 billion from Medicare, as provided in the Democrats' healthcare bill, would compromise the quality of care without guaranteeing the program's long-term solvency. However, since even President Obama's Health and Human Services Department doubts these cuts will be sustained, the most likely outcome is that the program continues hurtling toward insolvency.[11] In order to guarantee this vital program's survival, it needs to be overhauled comprehensively.

Political Power

Even before Medicare was created, President Johnson and congressional Democratic leaders understood that healthcare entitlements could easily be exploited for political gain. The idea was to make senior citizens, a key voting population, highly dependent on the government via entitlements, then demonize Republicans for opposing program expansions or even just advocating reforms. This cynical campaign has successfully driven a wedge between seniors and Republicans.

Evidence of the Democrats' long-term political strategy is available in President Johnson's White House phone recordings—the same recording system that produced the Watergate tapes which eventually forced Nixon from office. The Supreme Court ordered the Nixon tapes released during Watergate, but Johnson's tapes weren't released until 1993. And "Landslide Lyndon's" conversations revealed that a lot of raw political calculation underlay the creation of the Great Society entitlements.

Congressman Wilbur Mills working on the Medicare bill (Photo by Francis Miller/Time Life Pictures/Getty Images)

President Lyndon B. Johnson on the telephone in the Oval Office (Photo by Yoichi R. Okamoto)

For example, one telling conversation between congressional leaders and President Johnson occurred in 1965 following committee passage of the Medicare program. Ways and Means chairman Wilbur Mills told Johnson:

"I think we've got you something that we won't only run in '66 but here after."

The president's response, in part, was:

They [the Republicans] will work on us the rest of the year and this will be helpful.... There is a ready demand, and I know it, for this bill than all my other programs put together. And it will last longer.[12]

Johnson clearly welcomed Republican criticism over the bill. The program, he knew, would not only serve liberal ideology, but would be a powerful political weapon, regardless of its social consequences. Johnson understood that of all his Great Society programs, Medicare was his trump card. Once created it would be

President Lyndon B. Johnson and Majority Leader Carl Albert in the Oval Office
(Photo by Frank Wolfe)

politically impossible to re-write. Johnson, more than anyone, knew that Medicare would become an intractable feature of government and that its creation would give the Democratic Party a long-term political advantage.

During the same conversation, Johnson expressed concern about public review of the Medicare proposal, as well as potential opposition. He instructed Speaker John McCormack and Democratic majority leader Carl Albert to rush the bill through the House before anyone could raise objections:

> *Remember this. Nine out of ten things I get in trouble on, is because they lay around. It stinks. It's just like a dead cat on the door. When the committee reports it, you better either bury the cat or get some life into it. For God's sake don't let dead cats stand on your porch. You call that thing up [the Medicare bill] before they get their letters in [opposing the bill].*[13]

Democrats discussed the political advantages of Medicare in other venues as well. During House floor consideration of the bill, Carl Albert declared:

"*This bill will serve well those of us who support it, politically and otherwise, through the years.*"[14]

Indeed it has. Since passage in 1965, Medicare has become a key component of the Democrats' electoral strategy—just as Johnson, Albert, and Mills had predicted. Opposing crucial reforms for the program, which has grown from $64 million in 1966 to more than $430 billion in 2009, and expanding its rolls remain top priorities for Democrats today.[15] They simply refuse to recognize that America will soon be unable to pay for it.

Entitlement Tsunami

We are all victims of centralized control over key aspects of our economy. This was enabled by Democratic legislation, both major and minor, over the last sixty years. But Democrats never told Americans that the Great Society is unsustainable. Without reform, these entitlements will collapse under a wave a debt that has the potential to crush the entire economy.

With entitlements now consuming 60 percent of our year-to-year federal budget, the approaching entitlement tsunami is so large that it's beyond comprehension—$65 trillion[16]—and that doesn't even include the additional debt we'll wrack up from the Democrats' healthcare reform, once all the accounting tricks are exposed and rectified.

Reform is not an option; it's a necessity for our economic survival.

SOLUTION

In 2008, Congressman Paul Ryan introduced a bill called "A Roadmap for America's Future." Solving the crises of the Big Three, this legislation transforms our healthcare system, fixes Social Security, streamlines our tax code, and balances the budget.

Social Security

When they hear proposals to reform Social Security, most people immediately react with one question: "How would this affect me?" According to the American Roadmap, if you are fifty-five or older, there will be no changes in your Social Security or Medicare. Let me repeat that: for those fifty-five or older, your programs will not change. If you're under the age of fifty-five, however, you will receive ownership of your healthcare and retirement.

Politicians should easily understand how the American Roadmap fixes Social Security: the legislation sets up a structure of retirement nearly identical to what members of Congress and federal employees have today. All Americans would have their own personal account through which a portion of their Social Security taxes would be invested. Not only will everyone retire with more money, they'll also be able to pass this money along to their heirs—unlike Social Security, which leaves nothing for your children and grandchildren, no matter how much you paid into it or how little you collected.

So before politicians denounce this plan as "privatizing" Social Security, they should look in the mirror; what's good enough for them should be good enough for the American people.

Healthcare

The first step to reforming healthcare is to repeal the disastrous Democratic healthcare bill. We don't have trillions of dollars lying around to fund this scheme, whose central aim is to create millions of permanent Democratic voters who rely on the government's benevolence for their very lives. And even if we could afford it, the bill will only create an inefficient, bureaucratic, government-dominated health system. Free competition will be suppressed as the government uses a raft of subsidies and penalties to pick winners and losers among healthcare providers, patients, and related businesses. Private insurers will gradually transform into something resembling public utilities, with the government dictating their policies and prices.

There is a better way—one that actually *improves* healthcare, at a price we can afford. The American Roadmap reforms healthcare and achieves universal coverage largely through one simple measure: depending on your income level, a family of four will receive anywhere from $5,700 to $10,700 to purchase their own health insurance in any state.

The American Roadmap makes healthcare personalized, transparent, and affordable. When it comes to medical decisions, patients and doctors will be in control, not bureaucrats and insurance companies. If you like your current doctors and insurers, you can keep them. But there will also be a wide choice of alternatives, even for people with pre-existing conditions, who will have access to special state-based healthcare exchanges and high-risk pools. Furthermore, insurers will face pressure to keep prices low when people are allowed to buy their policies across state lines. And with this new program, you can keep your healthcare plan into retirement, so you can continue to choose your own doctor, treatment location, and other services you have been accustomed to throughout your life.

Finally, because of the relationship between trial lawyers and politicians in Washington, Congress has allowed lawyers far too big a role in the practice of medicine. So the American Roadmap will finally enact real tort reform to keep doctors with their patients and out of the courtrooms.

Politicians must be willing to walk through the fire and be honest with the American people about the mountain of debt that is bankrupting our country. The only way to stop this is to reform the Big Three by taking power away from Washington and putting it back in the hands of the individual.

Congressman Paul Ryan has devoted years of effort to developing "A Roadmap for America's Future." You can learn more about the plan at his website, www.americanroadmap.org.

CHAPTER FIVE

TAXES

*"The hardest thing in the world
to understand is the income tax."*
—Albert Einstein,
as quoted on the IRS website

BACKGROUND

AMERICA HAS SO MANY KINDS OF TAXES, IT'S HARD TO KEEP
track of them. At the federal level, we pay personal income taxes;
corporate income taxes; interest, dividend, and capital gains
taxes; and estate taxes. At the state and local levels, we are subject to personal and corporate income taxes; interest, dividend,
and capital gains taxes; estate taxes; sales taxes; and local property taxes. When federal, state, and local taxes are combined, some
Americans, depending on where they live, have to hand over
more than half their income to the government.

■ The federal income tax was enacted in 1913. While the tax
rate has varied, over time more and more families have

been exempted from income taxes entirely, meaning these taxes are collected from an ever-shrinking group of people. More than 36 percent of American taxpayers don't pay any income taxes.[1]

■ The federal taxation of corporate income began in 1909. Like personal income taxes, rates have varied, with a top rate of 35 percent today. The U.S. has the second highest corporate tax rate among developed nations when you combine federal and state taxes.

■ Taxes on investment income such as interest, dividends, and capital gains constitute double taxation: corporations pay income tax on profits, which are then distributed as dividends to shareholders and taxed yet again; similarly, taxes on interest and capital gains represent additional levies on after-tax income.

■ Known as the "death tax," the estate tax was created by the federal government in 1916 to tax the transfer of wealth and income after a person's death. This is also a form of double taxation, since the money is taxed when it is earned, and taxed again when it is passed on to someone else after the earner's death.

PROBLEM

Even the IRS admits our tax code is difficult to understand, which is why its website features the following quote from Albert Einstein:

"The hardest thing in the world to understand is the income tax."[2]

If Einstein had a hard time figuring out his taxes, what hope is there for the rest of us? The U.S. tax system is complex, unfair, inefficient, and economically damaging. It's so confusing that millions of Americans need assistance just filling out the forms.

- From 1955 to 2005, the number of words in the Internal Revenue Code and Regulations increased from 1.4 million to 9.1 million.[3]
- The IRS says Americans spend 7.6 billion hours each year sifting through tax forms at a cost of $193 billion a year.[4]
- Penalty provisions in the tax code have increased from some 14 in 1954 to more than 130 today; in other words, the government has created nearly ten times more ways to take your money from you.[5]

Forty percent of the federal government's revenue comes from payroll taxes. Most of the rest comes from federal income taxes, whose rates have varied drastically over time. The top rate was initially set at 7 percent in 1913, but this shot up to a whopping 94 percent by the Second World War. It stayed roughly at that level until President Kennedy lowered it to 70 percent, and it was later slashed to 28 percent by President Reagan. Today, the top rate is 35 percent, and is set to rise to 39.6 percent in 2011.[6]

Regardless of tax rates, the federal government has run a budget deficit for the better part of four decades, forcing us to borrow money and amass an unsustainable national debt now reaching $8.4 trillion.[7] This debt, much of which we owe to foreign governments, represents over 60 percent of our GDP and is rising.[8] Under current spending policies, we may soon join Zimbabwe, Lebanon, the Sudan, and other dysfunctional states whose debt tops 100 percent of GDP.

Contrary to what many politicians and bureaucrats say, we can't increase income taxes to balance the budget or pay down the federal debt. Today, those earning incomes above $32,879 (that is, the top 50 percent of taxpayers) already pay 97 percent of federal income taxes.[9] Tax rates on a couple earning $32,879, filing a joint tax return, would have to rise from 15 percent to 36.4 percent to balance the budget in 2010. For the top earners, the tax rate would have to rise from 35 percent to a staggering 84.9 percent.[10]

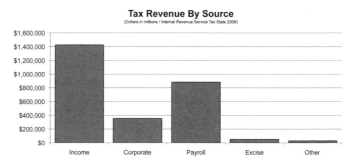

Only Japan boasts higher tax rates than the United States. Japan, like the United States, suffers from over-spending and has been unable to repay growing debt. (Internal Revenue Service, 2008 Tax Stats at a Glance)

Furthermore, even if tax rates went that high, it probably still wouldn't balance the budget. To the contrary, we could expect the government to collect *less* revenue, as Arthur Laffer showed in his famous "Laffer Curve." The curve demonstrates that if taxes go high enough, people work less and invest less—why work long hours and invest your money if Uncle Sam is just going to take your earnings? And if people work and invest less, there will be less money to tax and less government revenue. Likewise, lower tax rates actually create more tax revenue, because people work and invest more when they can keep more of what they earn. That's why lowering taxes while broadening the tax base is a key part of balancing the budget.

The Laffer Curve

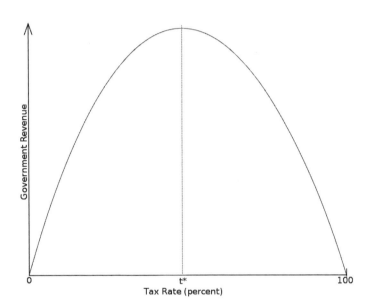

When I worked on a farm as a kid, I noticed that water moves along the path of least resistance. This is true whether it's flowing down a furrow to water a crop or out of a hose into a flower bed. The same can be said of financial capital, which flows through our economy to the point of least resistance—namely, to areas where the most profit can be made. I learned this lesson at an early age. When I was fourteen, I used my life savings to buy seven head of young cattle to raise and sell. I had two choices to feed them: buy feed, or fix fences in exchange for free grazing. Like water flowing down a furrow, my cattle went to pasture and I fixed fences so I could make a higher profit.

With its convoluted structure and counterproductive penalties for success, the U.S. tax system forces us along the path of greatest, not least, resistance. It's time to replace it with a system that empowers the people.

What Goes Unsaid

Many Americans can't understand why the Obama administration seems determined to spend our country into oblivion. They wonder whether the administration doesn't understand the danger or if they just don't care. Based on my experience as a member of the House Budget Committee, I can say with confidence that the administration both understands the problem and cares about it. It's just that they're rolling out their solution slowly, because it involves an unprecedented tax hike that the vast majority of Americans will vehemently oppose.

I realized the administration's strategy at a House Budget Committee meeting with Treasury Secretary Tim Geithner on February 24, 2010. Insisting we "don't have the luxury" of doing nothing to fix the budget, Geithner showed he understood our current fiscal situation is unsustainable. He proposed convening a commission, based on the Reagan-Greenspan Commission on Social Security, to develop recommendations for thoroughly reforming our fiscal policy.

To most observers, that probably seems like a reasonable idea. But I immediately understood that this commission, which is now meeting, was really meant to introduce the Obama administration's real fiscal "solution." This was explained with surprising bluntness in June 2009 during a private meeting between me, some other congressmen, and Paul Volcker, a White House advisor and former chairman of the Federal Reserve. In his eighties, Mr. Volcker looked tired that day as he discussed the federal budget in his capacity as chairman of the President's Economic Recovery Advisory Board. He didn't seem to realize there were Republicans in the room. Otherwise he probably would not have told us that in order to fund future obligations, balance the budget, and lower the national debt, the Obama administration believed the federal government would have to collect 25–30 percent of GDP in taxes.

Historically, the federal government has collected no more than 20 percent of GDP in taxes. So Volcker was outlining a staggering tax increase on the American people. Indeed, it would be so high a burden that it would be virtually impossible to collect it simply by raising income taxes and other existing taxes. The only feasible way of collecting this much tax revenue would be to introduce a European-style, national value-added tax (VAT)—similar to a national sales tax—*on top* of the federal income tax and all the other taxes we already pay.

Thus, I was unsurprised in April 2010 when Volker publicly suggested considering a VAT, as well as a new energy tax, in order to lower the deficit.[11] In an interview later that month, President Obama refused to rule out adopting the VAT. This contradicted his own spokesman, who insisted just before the interview that VAT is off the table.[12] Whether the administration ultimately tries to push through a VAT or not, it is desperately looking for a way to finance its spending binge—and higher taxes in some form or another will inevitably be a key part of the "solution."

SOLUTION

The Fair Tax for California

California is among the most regulated business environments in America. For example, some people thought chicken farming was cruel, so a 2008 law mandated free range chickens—virtually eliminating commercial egg farms, while driving chicken farms to other states and, ultimately, to foreign countries like Mexico (ironically, a country that allows cock fighting). Unsurprisingly, California also imposes one of the highest income tax rates in the United States—high taxes and suffocating regulation always seem to go together.

One reform that could bring business back to California is the Fair Tax. Championed in the House of Representatives by John Linder of Georgia, the Fair Tax would abolish *all* federal taxes and replace them with a national sales tax of 20–30 percent.

There's a lot of speculation as to how well the Fair Tax would work as a national tax system. While this question could use more research and debate, it's already clear the Fair Tax would have dramatic, immediate benefits if implemented in individual states. I asked the American Enterprise Institute (AEI) to study the feasibility of the Fair Tax as a replacement for California's byzantine, punitive tax system. California has one of the highest tax burdens in the country, yet still suffers from a revenue crisis. This is cause and effect; high taxes have contributed to California's relatively poor economic performance over the past few years, which in turn has eroded the state's revenue stream. The Laffer Curve is playing out in real-time in the Golden State, as lawmakers discover that rising taxes are not yielding more revenue.

In its analysis, AEI found that by slightly raising the state sales tax to around 10 percent and abolishing all other state taxes, California could generate the same amount of revenue it collects under the current complex system that taxes personal income, corporate income, sales, capital gains, and many other activities.[13] This reform would create a clear, transparent tax system that could fund government services, eliminate budget volatility, and help restore California as a business friendly state.

The benefits of the Fair Tax model are not limited to California; this model would solve the problems of many states currently suffering economic distress and financial insolvency. For California, if action is not taken soon, the chickens may be lucky they were run out of town before California's economy is completely fried.

A Roadmap to a Better Federal Tax System

America's federal income taxes also desperately need reform. Politicians often manipulate the tax law to benefit special interests, while everyday Americans get penalized when they work harder and achieve more success.

Here is the solution: we eliminate the tax code and replace it with a straightforward business tax as well as a personal income tax so simple you can file your taxes on a one-page form. The plan is spelled out in the American Roadmap:

- Individuals pay a flat income tax rate of either 10 percent or 25 percent depending on income and filing status.

- The corporate income tax is replaced with a Business Consumption Tax, similar to the Fair Tax, with an 8.5 percent tax on net business income.
- Taxes on interest, dividends, and capital gains are abolished, as well as the estate tax and the alternative minimum tax.

This reform would make the tax code simpler, fairer, more transparent, and less subject to abuse and political manipulation. It would immediately improve our economy while allowing American workers to keep more of the money they earn. What's more, anyone who prefers the current federal tax structure can stay in it—switching to the simplified, reformed code would be voluntary. I don't know many people who would *choose* to waste hours filling out all the current indecipherable tax forms or to pay lots of money for an accountant to do their taxes, but if that's your thing, I'm not going to stand in the way.

Of course, a lot of powerful people are vested in keeping everyone in the current system. So you can expect a lot of resistance to this commonsense reform from the usual quarters—the special interests, their favorite politicians, and big-government proponents. Additionally, one other big group will stridently oppose this reform: tax accountancy firms, which would lose millions every year if Americans could do their own taxes quickly and simply on a one-page form.

CHAPTER SIX

IMMIGRATION

*"Put the medical marijuana guy at one end
and start a strip club at the other."*
—a Turkish immigrant

BACKGROUND

IMMIGRANTS HAVE ALWAYS CONTRIBUTED TO AMERICA'S RICH
cultural heritage. From the birth of our country, nearly every U.S.
town, city, county, and state has held celebrations of cultural
heritage, from parades to festivals. American families who have
been here for generations celebrate alongside families who
have just arrived. It is uniquely American to recognize how immigrants strengthen, unite, and revitalize us. We have been the most
open country in world history, and we have been rewarded.

Today, however, our immigration system is broken, with an estimated 8 to 12 million people now living illegally in the United
States. The chaos along our border has allowed drugs and gangs to

enter our country with impunity. In response, Congress has increased the number of Border Patrol agents along our southern border from 3,555 in 1992 to 20,119 in 2009, and it has boosted the number of Border Patrol agents covering all our borders to 20,202.[1] Yet the problems of illegal immigration, drugs, and gangs continue unabated. Adding more Border Patrol agents is clearly not a long-term solution to the chronic problems along our borders.

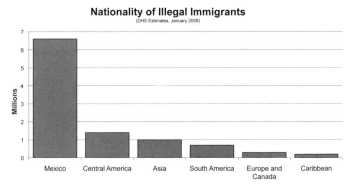

Nationality of Illegal Immigrants
(DHS Estimates, January 2009)

Illegal immigrants are estimated to number from 8 to 12 million. Long, relatively uncontrolled borders along the Mexican and Canadian frontier have made illegal entry easy in the past. While security is improving, the borders are not secure. (U.S. Department of Homeland Security, Office of Immigration Statistics, January 2009)

But there is a solution. If we can set aside the red-hot emotions that infuse this issue, we'll see we can fix our broken immigration system, restore the rule of law, protect our economy, and defend our borders and ports of entry. And we can do it without resorting to measures that damage our reputation as a welcoming country to people from all over the world.

PROBLEM

Some of my favorite Americans to talk to are new Americans. Immigrants' stories of how they came to our shores can be educational, uplifting, and sobering. Their love for America always inspires me.

Here's an example: I was having dinner in late 2009 with a Turk, a Pole, a Hungarian, and an Italian. (No, this isn't the start of a bad joke.) All four were worried and confused about America's future—worried because of the direction the federal government is heading, and confused because they couldn't believe the country they and their families came to is beginning to resemble the countries they left.

My friend who fled Communist Poland observed:

"What this government is doing has been tried before in Poland under the Communists. They promised to take care of everyone and make everybody equal. But they bankrupted the country."

My Hungarian friend agreed, saying:

"The Communists promised everything and delivered a dictatorship."

I know my Hungarian friend's story well because he's my neighbor in California. After World War II, as the Iron Curtain came down on Eastern Europe, Hungary came under Soviet control. Hungarian Communists backed by Moscow claimed they would build a workers' utopia, but they built instead an oppressive political system enforced by Soviet tanks. The only people who benefitted from this system were Communist Party leaders and their Soviet bosses.

Facing a hopeless future, during the 1970s my friend tried unsuccessfully for four years to escape. But at least he survived;

he had friends who were shot by border guards or blown up by land mines while trying to flee to Austria. He eventually decided on another strategy: he became a doctor and began to lobby the local Communist bureaucrats to allow him to go to Austria for additional training. They let him go as long as he left his wife and child behind, a standard tactic used by Communist regimes to prevent defections.

He explained to me once with tears in his eyes that the political oppression was so bad in Hungary and the economy so weak that even doctors struggled to support their families. So he agreed with his wife that he would defect and then try to get his family to the United States. He succeeded, but he wasn't reunited with his family for nearly a decade.

My friend, who has now delivered thousands of babies in my hometown, is thankful he had a place where he could bring his family and earn a good living as a doctor. But that night at dinner he also told us he was worried about America's future. The Obama administration's socialist policies in healthcare and other realms, he said, remind him of Communist Hungary.

At that dinner, the Italian lamented California's crumbling economy and its effect on his construction business, saying:

"The only interest I have had in anyone renting my vacant buildings was some guy that called last week who wanted a facility to dispense medical marijuana."

Referring to the historic Tagus Ranch (which was made famous by John Steinbeck in *The Grapes of Wrath* and is located nearby where I grew up and still live), the Turk responded:

"You should buy the old abandoned building and put the medical marijuana guy at one end and start a strip club at the other. Both busi-

nesses attract cash customers so at least you could hide some money from
the government before they take everything."

"Just like Eastern Europe under the Communists," the Pole
observed dejectedly.

That conversation was certainly colorful, but not unusual.
Many immigrants across the country have expressed similar
concerns to me. America is changing and losing its special place
in the world. Our leaders are becoming like socialists everywhere
on earth, seeking greater and greater government control, massive
welfare states, high taxes, and limits to economic and political
freedom.

America's socialization was also mentioned to me regretfully
by a Russian immigrant friend who grew up under Soviet
Communism. Still another friend from El Salvador, who for
years fought Communists financed by Cuba and the Soviet
Union in the mountains outside of San Salvador, shared similar
concerns—that many of the things the Communists had said
back home in the 1980s are being repeated by officials in
Washington today. Each man had watched as the promise of a
socialist utopia in his home country gave way to oppression, murder, and economic collapse. Communist Party hacks, secret
police, and the military ran the government, subjecting the people to totalitarian control.

These are what I call real immigrant stories. I've heard count-
less others from around the world. They should remind Americans
why our country is a beacon of hope for so many people trapped in
poverty and oppression, and they should serve as a warning about
the direction in which this country is heading. Sadly, these stories
are drowned out in the shrillness of the immigration debate.

Gerrypandering

Immigration is a hot topic today. Many new Americans wonder how a country so open to immigrants could sour on its legacy. We must not allow this to happen. America must stay open to people who seek freedom and a better way of life—people who will contribute immensely to our country's prosperity.

Immigrants are not the problem. The problem is the federal government's failure to secure our border and develop a rational immigration policy that meets our economic needs. In the meantime, politicians cynically exploit the issue for political gain.

Many Democrats pander to the emotions of the Mexican-American community by promising amnesty for illegal immigrants—a promise they know they can't keep. This is a crass attempt to increase Hispanic support for Democratic candidates. To seal the deal, they also promise free education, free healthcare, and better wages as long as Hispanics keep voting Democrat. I call this "gerrypandering" because it draws rhetorical boundaries to deliver votes.

Despite the Democrats' big congressional majorities and control of the White House, they have not fulfilled their promises on immigration. President Bush supported comprehensive reform to fix the broken immigration system in 2006, but the Democrats refused to work with him. Here's why: although some Democrats campaigned on false promises of amnesty, many other Democrats promised to kick illegal immigrants out of the country. They even cynically attacked Republicans for being soft on illegal immigration. That's a bit of recent political history the national Democratic Party doesn't like to mention.

SOLUTION

Congress should write new immigration and border security legislation and send it to the president to sign or veto. Only then will we truly know who wants to fix the broken system and who doesn't. No more gerrypandering.

Protecting our southern border from drug cartels and gangs is our first priority and a basic constitutional responsibility of our government. The key to border security is not more fences, police, and border patrol agents, but the agency of government the Founding Fathers intended to protect us: the U.S. military. We need the secretary of defense to develop, in consultation with other agencies, a plan for the military to protect our borders and ports from criminal activity. After visiting our military servicemen and women several times in Iraq and Afghanistan, I can tell you their technology, know-how, and equipment are more than enough to secure our borders.

We also have to remove politicians' excuses for inaction. One of the most common excuses for not militarizing the border is that we're prevented from doing so by the Posse Comitatus Act (USC, Title 18. Part I. Chapter 67. Section 1385), which states:

> *Whoever, except in cases and under circumstances expressly authorized by the Constitution or Act of Congress, willfully uses any part of the Army or the Air Force as a posse comita-tus or otherwise to execute the laws shall be fined under this title or imprisoned not more than two years, or both.*

Note that the Act explicitly authorizes Congress to carve exceptions to it. And Congress has repeatedly done so, especially for itself. For example, the FBI may request military assistance to investigate the assassination, kidnapping, or assault of a member of Congress. Moreover, the government can use our Armed Forces to protect some of our national parks and federal timber in Florida. So if Congress can carve out exemptions for itself and for Florida trees, it can do so to protect our borders. What's more, the Act can also be suspended to protect our country from terrorists, which is a growing concern along the southern border.

Mexico needs our help, too. It is at war with drug cartels and other vicious criminals who routinely massacre innocent people. In one particularly despicable crime, a drug cartel in early 2010 slaughtered the family of a soldier just after he lost his life helping to track down and kill a top drug kingpin. More than 15,000 Mexicans have been killed in drug-related violence since 2006, and the violence has begun to spill over the border.[2] As our friend, ally, and largest trading partner, Mexico deserves our help in crushing the drug cartels that threaten both our countries.

The best thing we can do to help Mexico is to stop the cartels' flow of drugs, money, and personnel across our border. If we deploy a military surge on the border like we did in Iraq, we'll severely disrupt the smuggling operations whose profits provide the cartels' lifeblood.

Guest Workers

I've lived among immigrants my whole life. One fallacy that's often heard in Washington, D.C., is that once people get to America, they never return to their country of origin. Nearly all immigrants are proud of the "old country" and its heritage. They often leave behind parents, grandparents, aunts, and uncles, and in some cases wives and children. Nearly every recent immigrant I've met longs to visit his or her homeland. Many even dream of making their old country more like America, though you rarely hear about that from pandering politicians. Illegal immigrants also want to visit their home countries but, of course, they're afraid if they do they won't be able to make it back to America.

Keep that in mind when you consider the "touchback provision," a proposed alternative to amnesty for illegal immigrants. Touchback means that someone in this country illegally would have to leave the country and return the legal way. This is a sensible, feasible, and just measure that should be part of any comprehensive solution, though politicians demagogue the proposal to deliberately stoke fear. Although some claim illegal immigrants would ignore touchback, the truth is, most would welcome the opportunity to visit their homeland if there were a fair system through which they could come back to America legally for work. Remember, many illegal immigrants have not seen their families back home for years.

Most Americans welcome immigrants but also want law and order, as well as protections against immigrants taking jobs, lowering wages, and collecting welfare. When we have a growing economy with lots of available jobs, this usually isn't a problem. And even in today's troubled economy, you find fewer and fewer American citizens willing to work as agricultural laborers, landscapers, roofers, or in other low-wage jobs. So the key is matching foreigners that want to work in the United States with employers willing to take responsibility for them. Many countries in the Middle East, Europe, Australia, and New Zealand have this kind of program that matches guest workers with jobs. Even Russia has one. The United States can do the same.

Here are a few questions everyday people typically ask me about a guest worker program:

- *Who would be eligible for a work visa?* Anyone who is sponsored by an American employer, enters the United States from his own country, has no criminal record or health issues, and has had proper immunization shots.
- *Who pays for the work visa and the transportation to the United States?* The employer pays.
- *How will you verify employees are legal?* Employers would be required to use a new system of tamper-proof identification cards.
- *Wouldn't it take a long time for this program to work?* Yes; that's why there will be a 7-year phase-in before heavy penalties take effect.
- *Would people here illegally really leave under a touchback provision?* Yes; immigrants overwhelmingly want to visit their home countries and would do so if they could return to America legally for work.
- *Is it necessary for the U.S. military to secure the border if this new verifiable system is in place?* Yes, but the military wouldn't be there to patrol. Remember, immigrants will now be using the front door, crossing through the border at the normal entry points, where they will deal with the border patrol. The military will be there to protect us from terrorists, drug dealers, and gang bangers, consistent with the vision of the Founding Fathers.

Tackling immigration reform must be more than a partisan political exercise. As American author and poet Henry David Thoreau once said:

"A thousand hacking at the branches of evil is worth nothing to one strike at the root."

I have outlined a simple, 3-step reform that strikes at the root of our nation's immigration problem—militarize the border, pass a touchback provision, and approve a guest worker program. This plan punishes criminals, protects the American people, and establishes a just system of immigration.

America has always been a place of shelter for the huddled masses of the world. We should be proud of the beacon of hope shining from our country and be compassionate to those who seek to come here. After all, the only thing worse than having a porous border is having a porous border that no one wants to cross because no one wants to come to your country.

CHAPTER SEVEN

EDUCATION

*"We have the power because there are more
than 3.2 million people who are willing to
pay us hundreds of millions of dollars."*
—National Education Association
General Counsel Bob Chanin

BACKGROUND

IN 1965, PRESIDENT LYNDON JOHNSON SIGNED THE ELEMENTARY
and Secondary Education Act, the largest expansion of the federal
government's role in public education since the founding of our
Republic. The law provided federal funds for schools with low-
income children, for state government education programs, and
for education instructional materials, training, and research.

Since the Act's adoption, Democratic leaders in Congress have
consistently worked to increase the scope of federal control over
our nation's education system. They received some help from
Republicans in 2002 when Congress passed the No Child Left
Behind Act, which eclipsed the 1965 law as the most significant
expansion of federal control over our nation's schools. No Child

Left Behind was meant to shift the federal focus away from micro-managing schools toward a more constructive role providing financial incentives that would reward educational success and punish failure. Nationwide standardized testing was introduced to measure success rates, but state and local governments were to keep the power to tailor their programs to meet local needs. Most important, parents would be allowed to transfer their kids out of chronically failing schools.

When Congress first expanded Washington's role in public education, there were some 42 million public school students in the United States, and national spending on education was approximately $40 billion. Today, there are 49 million students attending public schools at a cost of more than $1 trillion. Overall, spending per pupil has grown from an average of $375 to $10,041.[1] At the same time, American academic achievement has declined relative to the rest of the developed world. Today, across the country, public education is consigning our children to unsafe and ineffective public schools.

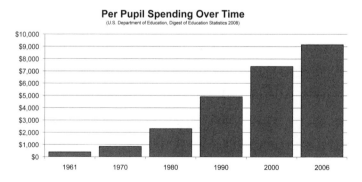

Per Pupil Spending Over Time
(U.S. Department of Education, Digest of Education Statistics 2008)

Per pupil spending has risen dramatically in the United States. In 1960, $375 per year covered the education of a child. Today we spend more than $10,000. (U.S. Department of Education, Digest of Educational Statistics 2008)

PROBLEM

America's public schools are failing, especially in some of our biggest cities. In Detroit, Michigan, for example, taxpayers pay $11,112 per public school student, well above the national average.[2] And yet, despite the federal government providing around 18 percent of the funding—also well above the national average—Detroit's graduation rate is a dismal 25 percent.[3] The situation is even worse in Washington, D.C., which has the nation's worst performing schools; shockingly, one in four D.C. public school students has been threatened on campus with a deadly weapon.[4]

Public education advocates typically blame these failures on insufficient education funding. Many of the worst schools, however, spend the highest amount per pupil on education; and some, like Detroit, draw high levels of federal support.

Meanwhile, schools with high-achieving students and high graduation rates typically spend at or below the national average. For example, Mesa Unified School District in Arizona spends just $5,932 per student, but has a 77 percent graduation rate.[5]

Higher spending clearly has not helped troubled schools achieve academic excellence. In Washington, D.C., per pupil spending was $11,000 in 2008 while graduation rates were just 47 percent. A nearby big city, Baltimore, achieved that same graduation rate while spending just $8,000 per student. And Atlanta, a city similar to Washington and Baltimore in both demographics and poverty levels, has attained a 61 percent graduation rate spending just $6,000 per student.[6]

So if it isn't inadequate spending, why are so many public schools failing our children? The D.C. Opportunity Scholarship Program provides a case study that helps answer that question.

D.C. Opportunity Scholarships

In our nation's capital, parents were desperate for change. One of the worst school districts in the nation had taken its toll on generations of residents, and few believed things would improve under the D.C. education establishment.

Many top government officials live with their families in Washington. But they don't have to send their own kids to Washington's terrible public schools—they can afford top-tier private schools like Sidwell Friends, where generations of presidents including President Obama have sent their children.[7] A few years ago, everyday parents in D.C. appealed to the government for the same opportunity—they wanted to transfer their kids from unsafe, failing schools to good schools.

In 2004, Congress agreed to deliver meaningful school choice to district residents with the Opportunity Scholarship Program, which provided participants with vouchers toward paying tuition at a private school of their choice. Republican leaders enacted the program despite intense opposition by Democratic leaders and the National Education Association. The vouchers became enormously popular, giving several thousand low-income families a chance for quality education. The U.S. Department of Education concluded that the program offered measurable increases in academic achievement. Parents and students testified that the program provided kids with a safe environment where teachers and students were committed to education.

The vouchers' popularity grew in a community dominated by Democrats and public sector unions—sectors that are hostile to school choice. But the District's mayor and Superintendant of Public Instruction, both Democrats, as well as the Democrat-dominated D.C. city council strongly supported the program, citing superior outcomes as well as lower cost, which was roughly half the cost of attending a D.C. public school.

Sadly, once Democrats gained control of Congress, the program's days were numbered. School choice threatens an influential Democratic constituency, the teachers' unions, whose members would face more direct competition from private schools. Meanwhile, Democrats oppose school choice for ideological reasons—they want to keep people dependent on government-run schools. So in 2009 Democrats in Congress passed legislation quietly killing the program, and President Obama signed the bill.[8] It was a shameful surrender to partisan politics without any policy justification. And the real victims are thousands of poor children whose chance at a good education was sacrificed on the altar of Washington politics.

Union Power vs. Children

The National Education Association (NEA) is the nation's largest teacher's union. It is devoted to protecting teachers' salaries and benefits, not to promoting children's welfare. A vigorous defender of the status quo in education, the NEA especially opposes reform efforts that would empower parents and students with school choice. NEA general counsel Bob Chanin clarified his union's priorities during a 2009 gathering in Washington, D.C., as he discussed why the NEA is so effective:

> *Despite what some among us would like to believe, it is not because of our creative ideas. It is not because of the merit of our positions. It is not because we care about children. And*

it is not because we have a vision of a great public school for every child. NEA and its affiliates are effective advocates because we have power. And we have power because there are more than 3.2 million people who are willing to pay us hundreds of millions of dollars in dues each year because they believe that we are the union that can most effectively represent them—the union that can protect their rights and advance their interests as education employees.[9]

This outrageous, selfish statement garnered a standing ovation from the NEA members in attendance. Unsurprisingly, the remarks went virtually unreported in the mainstream media, which falsely portray the education establishment as an impartial advocate for children. As Chanin's statement shows, the simple truth is that the education establishment, as represented by organizations like the NEA, pursues its own interests, which are often incompatible with those of our children.

When parents and students have school choice, they naturally flock to the best schools. And when families are given the opportunity to take responsibility for their kids' education, when quality is demanded, and when students are afforded a safe learning environment, academic achievement flourishes. But the NEA is trapping our children in failing schools solely to defend its own power.

American Academic Stagnation and Global Competition

It takes effort to achieve the kind of innovation that has driven America's economy and attracted investment from around the world. Previous generations of Americans toiled to solve complex problems, often leveraging scarce resources and suffering long hours for modest gain. This drive for discovery and innovation stemmed from the American spirit of entrepreneurship, made possible by a passion for science and a desire to understand the world around us.

Today, American students are falling behind in math, science, and other key subjects. Thirty-nine percent of high school seniors cannot answer basic algebra and geometry questions, and 46 percent cannot answer basic questions related to earth science, biology, or chemistry.[10] Yet more Americans than ever are attending some form of college. One might ask, "What are American students learning?"

The unfortunate truth is that our colleges and universities are graduating more lawyers and liberal arts majors than doctors or scientists, forcing the United States to import physicians, technicians, and other experts. If this trend continues, it will erode the educational edge we need to sustain our pace of scientific and technological innovation. Meanwhile, rising economic powerhouses like China and India are aggressively training their populations in key technological and scientific fields. These foreign powers are eager to exploit our educational shortcomings in order to gain long-term economic and military superiority.

SOLUTION

As Congress considers further education reforms, it needs to recognize the immense damage the American education system has suffered at the hands of the federal government, which has taken decision making away from local schools, parents, and teachers, and centralized it in Washington, D.C. Federal legislators need to understand that funding rightly remains mostly a local and state responsibility, and so too should education policy. Less than 10 percent of overall education funding comes from the federal government, yet with each dollar comes the temptation to micromanage and a growing risk of dependence.[11] The federal role in education was significantly increased with the No Child Left Behind Act which, though well-intentioned, should be rolled back in favor of local control. And the remaining federal role should concentrate on developing knowledge in the subjects that will keep America globally competitive, particularly math and science.

Congress also needs to understand that despite the constant calls for more education spending, there is no evidence that a lack of funds is a critical problem. Today, we are spending the highest per pupil dollars in communities with the lowest academic achievement. Rather than simply throwing more money into the black hole of bureaucratic public education and its debilitating unions, we should provide financial support directly to students.

School choice should not be limited to the rich and powerful as it largely is today, when members of Congress are more than three times as likely as the average American to send their children to private schools.[12] Furthermore, many of the most vocal Democratic lawmakers attended private schools themselves and now send their children to private schools. What is good for government elites should be good for everyday Americans.

To end this disparity, Congress should not only restore the D.C. Choice Scholarship Program, but expand it into a national education voucher program operating in all fifty states. All future federal education funding could then be tied directly to students.

Such a program would force schools, teachers, and other academic organizations to compete for their jobs, not lobby Congress for them. It would restore local control to education and create meaningful choice for parents and students. Of course, power brokers in Washington, especially the NEA, will fight the reform. But at some point, Democratic lawmakers will have to stand up to the unions or surrender their jobs to new leaders who will finally put our children's interests first.

Another crucial reform is to expand our great community college system, most of which is governed by local boards that are accountable to the voters. I served six years on one of those boards for a community college in my area. An excellent supplement to high school learning, community colleges need to improve access by creating programs targeting high school juniors and seniors. In fact, every high school student should either be in a college prep program or be earning credit through a community college. Greater access and opportunity to community college programs will open the doors to early career and vocational educational opportunities.

This does not require any federal legislation. Junior colleges can work with local school districts to create these programs. This is why in the Republic created by our Founding Fathers, we elected school boards that are accountable to the people; the remote federal government doesn't understand the needs of local communities.

Overall, the solution to America's education challenge is to empower students, parents, and teachers, not bureaucrats or politicians in Washington, D.C.

CHAPTER EIGHT

FOREIGN POLICY

*"Our doubts are traitors and make us lose the
good we oft might win by fearing to attempt."*
—a quotation framed on
Admiral Hyman Rickover's wall

BACKGROUND

MOST AMERICANS RECOGNIZE THE DATES OF SEPTEMBER 11, 2001,
and December 7, 1941, when the United States was attacked by
radical Muslims and the Japanese air force, respectively. There is
another date worth remembering, too. On August 24, 1814,
British troops marched into Washington, D.C., and set fire to the
U.S. Capitol, the president's mansion, and other federal buildings.
It was the most egregious attack of the War of 1812. As a seven-
year-old girl recalled:

*"At first I thought the world was on fire. Such a flame I have
never seen."[1]*

All but one of the city's federal buildings were razed in the fire,
which also destroyed the 3,000 books belonging to the Library of

Congress. Only a torrential rainstorm saved the capital from complete destruction. In fact, afterward there was talk of moving our capital to a more secure location. The attack came just three decades after the end of the Revolutionary War, when America had signed the Treaty of Paris with Great Britain.

After Washington was rebuilt, America was safe from foreign attack until the Japanese bombed Pearl Harbor more than a century later. Thus, an unprepared America was brutally forced into the Second World War just over two decades after we had fought the First World War—a conflict heralded as "the war to end all wars." Like the 1814 attack on Washington, D.C., the destruction at Pearl Harbor was colossal. The Japanese air force decimated the U.S. Navy's battleship force: five of eight battleships were destroyed and the rest damaged; several other ships were also destroyed, as were most of our combat planes in Hawaii. More than 2,400 Americans were killed in the attack.[2]

The Second World War transformed the United States from a bastion of isolationism into a global superpower with the world's strongest military. To prevent another worldwide cataclysm, we took on the burden of defending and spreading freedom and democracy throughout the world. This was perhaps most profoundly realized in the transformed capitals of our former fascist enemies—Tokyo, Rome, and the parts of Berlin we and our allies controlled.

America had dedicated precious blood and treasure to defeating fascism, yet freedom was betrayed again when the Soviet Union put Eastern Europe under Communist despotism and threatened much of the rest of the world. It took more than forty years, trillions of dollars, and eight American administrations to defeat the brutal Soviet dictatorship.

With the fall of the Berlin Wall in 1989 and the collapse of the Soviet Union in 1991, many Americans once again thought our nation's safety had been secured and that freedom and democracy had finally triumphed. While the threat of Soviet-backed Communism had ended, however, America still had plenty of enemies in the world, even if we weren't paying much attention to them. Freedom was about to be betrayed once again.

We had our first glimpse of the evil, destructive intent of our new adversaries just two years after the collapse of the Soviet Union, when Islamist terrorists bombed the World Trade Center in February 1993. Like clockwork, attacks followed on our troops stationed in Saudi Arabia (1996), our embassies in Kenya and Tanzania (1998), and the USS *Cole* docked in Yemen (2000). None of those attacks raised much alarm, however. It was only after the World Trade Center and Pentagon were attacked on September 11, 2001, that Americans were jolted into realizing the magnitude of the threat to our country.

PROBLEM

We confront many threats around the world today, Islamic extremism being the most potent. And there are far more threats than most people realize; some plots are quietly thwarted by U.S. law enforcement and intelligence services without the public even hearing of them. Overall, thanks to the courage and dedication of our men and women in the armed forces, the U.S. mainland has not suffered a successful attack since 2001.

In addition to war spending, we spend over $700 billion a year on national security and foreign affairs to ensure attacks like those in 1814, 1941, and 2001 don't reoccur. By necessity, this involves spreading democracy and freedom abroad—the best defense against attack, as well as a powerful expression of American values. Additionally, America helps other countries through foreign aid and through countless acts of compassion by private institutions, non-profits, and caring individuals. For example, former presidents George H. W. Bush and Bill Clinton teamed up in 2005 to raise private money for tsunami relief in Southeast Asia. More recently, Presidents George W. Bush and Bill Clinton undertook a similar campaign to aid victims of the earthquake in Haiti.

When necessary, we have even made the ultimate sacrifice—the lives of our citizens—to defend freedom and democracy around the world. These sacrifices are marked with memorials

Pictured above is the 42.5-acre Aisne-Marne Cemetery and Memorial in France. It contains the graves of 2,289 war dead, as well as the inscription of 1,060 names of missing American soldiers. The American Battle Monuments Commission administers, operates, and maintains twenty-four permanent American burial grounds on foreign soil that inter 124,909 U.S. war dead. (The American Battle Monuments Commission)

both here at home and around the world. Such is the case, for example, in Normandy, where a permanent memorial commemorates Americans who gave their lives to liberate Europe from Nazi control. There are also 124,909 American soldiers buried in cemeteries around the world, whose graves form their own monument to American sacrifice.

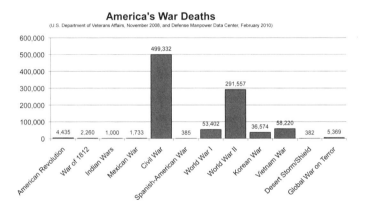

America's War Deaths
(U.S. Department of Veterans Affairs, November 2008, and Defense Manpower Data Center, February 2010)

To honor the memory of these fallen heroes and to protect the liberty for which they fought and died, Americans must remain vigilant in recognizing and eliminating threats to our freedom. Merely reacting to attacks will not suffice in an age of potential dirty bombs, biological attacks, and other weapons of mass destruction. We need an offensive strategy that dedicates funds and manpower to spreading freedom, attacking our enemies, and keeping America and her allies safe—because freedom can always be betrayed again.

Middle East

Global dependence on Middle Eastern oil, particularly from Saudi Arabia and Iran, enables the financing of international terrorism. And our own reliance on foreign oil makes us less safe; our 2009 trade deficit was $517 billion, almost half of which comprised imported oil. Oil exporting countries are now the fourth largest holders of U.S. Treasury securities.

Our dependence on Saudi oil is particularly threatening. Saudi Arabia has been home since the eighteenth century to Wahhabism, a radical sect of Sunni Islam. Although most Muslims around the world are Sunnis, historically very few practice Saudi-style Islam. Yet Western dependence on Saudi oil has given the Saudis an outsized influence in world affairs along with the financial means to spread Wahhabism throughout much of the world; Saudi Arabia has funded some 1,500 mosques, 210 Islamic centers, 202 colleges, and 2,000 schools in countries that do not have a Muslim majority.[3] And the ideology they're spreading isn't pretty, as was discovered in a 2005 Freedom House survey of Wahhabi literature in American mosques and Islamic centers:

> The Wahhabism that the Saudi monarchy enforces, and on which it bases its legitimacy, is shown in these documents as a fanatically bigoted, xenophobic and sometimes violent ideology. These publications articulate its wrathful dogma, rejecting the coexistence of different religions and explicitly condemning Christians, Jews, all other non-Muslims, as well as non-Wahhabi Muslims. The various Saudi publications gathered for this study state that it is a religious obligation for Muslims to hate Christians and Jews and warn against imitating,

befriending, or helping such "infidels" in any way, or taking part in their festivities and celebrations. They instill contempt for America because the United States is ruled by legislated civil law rather than by totalitarian Wahhabi-style Islamic law. Some of the publications collected for this study direct Muslims not to take American citizenship as long as the country is ruled by infidels and tells them, while abroad, above all, to work for the creation of an Islamic state.[4]

Wahhabism spreads Islamic extremism, which in turn breeds terrorism; it's no coincidence that fifteen of the nineteen 9/11 hijackers were Saudis, along with Osama bin Laden himself. Other Middle Eastern nations breed fanatics, of course, but the Saudis stand alone in dedicating the massive resources of their oil wealth toward turning out Islamic extremists. To this day, every time Americans gas up their cars, they are financing the spread of radical Islam.

Aside from al Qaeda and the Saudis, we also face the threat of state-sponsored terrorism by Iran. In 1979, the secular Shah was overthrown by religious fanatics who practice Shia Islam. Since then, the so-called "Islamic Republic of Iran" has been a theocracy run by corrupt clerics and government thugs. The regime poses a significant threat to the Middle East and beyond: they have vowed to destroy Israel; they are building nuclear weapons; and they lend military assistance to terrorist groups in Iraq and Afghanistan to attack U.S. troops, and to Hamas in the Gaza Strip and Hezbollah in Lebanon to attack Israel.

Iranians, particularly young people, have recently protested in the streets against the clerics and the totalitarian government.

In June 2009, hundreds of thousands of Iranians protested the rigged results of a presidential election "won" by the unhinged Mahmoud Ahmadinejad. The unrest was the largest since demonstrations against the Shah in the 1970s. The brave protestors, however, received no meaningful assistance—and barely even an encouraging word—from the Obama administration, which feared that backing the Iranian people would hurt Obama's goal of "engaging" the Iranian regime. Predictably, government thugs brutally put down the protests.

Central and South America

We previously discussed the threat we face from the smuggling of drugs and people across our southern border, which now resembles a war zone. For example, the Mexican City of Juarez, just across the border from El Paso, is currently the murder capital of the world, with an average of seven murder victims per day.

Dominating the illegal drug market in the United States, Mexican drug traffickers are forming partnerships with U.S. gangs. Between 545 and 707 metric tons of cocaine come to the United States every year from South America, with 90 percent of that supply coming from Columbia and the rest largely originating in Bolivia and Peru.[5]

The preferred drug smuggling routes to Mexico are the eastern Pacific and western Caribbean routes. The drugs are transported by planes, boats, or even makeshift submarines through Central America. Once in Mexico, cocaine crosses our porous southern border anywhere from California to Texas. Recently, Venezuela has become the primary transit country for moving Colombian cocaine by non-commercial aircraft.

Despite being the world's biggest cocaine producer, Colombia is a staunch U.S. ally surrounded by anti-American, leftwing governments like those in Venezuela, Nicaragua, Bolivia, and Ecuador. Under outgoing President Alvaro Uribe, the Colombian government has made enormous strides in defeating the leftist guerillas and narco-paramilitaries that have blighted Colombia for years. Uribe has also improved human rights, partnered with the United States to fight cocaine trafficking, and has strongly advocated free trade with the United States.

This is a stark contrast to Venezuela under the dictatorship of Hugo Chavez. Chavez doesn't look to Thomas Jefferson for inspiration, but to that old Communist in Havana, Fidel Castro. He's also facilitated suspicious activities in South America by his allies in Iran. For example, Hezbollah, the Lebanon-based terrorist organization backed by the Iranian government, is widely believed to have set up terrorist cells in Venezuela under Chavez.

Communist dictator Hugo Chavez (right) meets with Iranian President and anti-American ally Mahmoud Ahmadinejad (left) at the Miraflores presidential palace in Caracas on November 25, 2009. (Photo by Juan Barreto/AFP/Getty Images)

We've seen this story before; in the 1980s, the Communist government in Nicaragua allowed numerous terrorist organizations to establish a presence in the country in order to further global terrorism. We can expect the same from the likes of Chavez and his allies. In fact, in March 2010 a Spanish judge who was trying terrorism suspects accused Chavez of collaborating with ETA, a Spanish terrorist group, and with FARC, a Columbian narco-terrorist organization. At the same time, the U.S. State Department's annual report on drug trafficking accused Venezuelan security forces of "directly assisting" Colombian guerrillas linked to cocaine smuggling.[6]

Official sponsorship of terrorist groups in Latin America constitutes a major threat to the United States, since terrorists can easily cross our southern border with the assistance of Latin American gangs and other criminal organizations.

I discussed this disturbing prospect and other security concerns in a January 2009 meeting with Mexican President Felipe Calderon. We met at the U.S. Capitol, along with Speaker Pelosi and other Democratic leaders. Two other Republicans and I represented House Republican leader John Boehner.

After the usual diplomatic pleasantries, I expected an informative discussion of the chaos on our border, Mexico's gang and drug violence, and the Mexican government's brave crackdown on drug cartels. So I was shocked when the first Democrat to speak ignored these issues, instead bemoaning the lack of union membership in Mexico. The next Democrat also addressed an irrelevant issue—Mexico's lax environmental laws.

Finally, the following Democratic speaker mentioned the violence in Mexico—but he blamed it on U.S. gun laws. In other words, the Second Amendment to our Constitution was responsible for the near civil war in Mexico between drug gangs and the government.

I was dismayed that America's congressional leaders would use this opportunity to advance leftwing policies in Mexico, considering the appalling situation there. President Calderon and the Mexican people have lost friends, family, soldiers, and police in their war against the cartels. So when it was my turn to speak. I told President Calderon:

> *Mr. President, I know you are experiencing tough times in your country. I just want you to know that we stand ready to help you as you try to rid your country of drug violence and criminal gangs.*

Leaving that meeting, I was embarrassed for our country's leaders and seriously worried about the future of our Republic. It's the responsibility of congressional leaders to promote our national interests, not to lecture foreign leaders about union membership, environmental regulations, or the supposed deficiencies of our own gun laws. It was then that I fully realized that the radical left has gained full control over our nation's leadership.

This was apparent when President Calderon addressed the Congress almost year and a half later on May 20, 2010. Clearly remembering what was told to him at that meeting in the Capitol, Calderon declared to Congress that American gun laws contributed to the violence in Mexico.

Africa: The Forgotten Continent

In 2009, U.S. foreign aid to Africa amounted to around $6.6 billion, distributed to forty-seven countries.[7] This aid included programs such as the "Women's Justice and Empowerment Initiative," "President's Malaria Initiative," "African Education Initiative," "Congo Basin Forest Partnership," "Africa Global Competitiveness Initiative," and "Initiative to End Hunger in Africa."[8]

More than half the funding went to health-related programs to address epidemics of malaria, HIV/AIDS, and other diseases. HIV/AIDS has been particularly devastating in Sub-Saharan Africa, home to more than 67 percent of the world's HIV/AIDS infected population. In total, an estimated 33.4 million people are infected with the disease worldwide. Over half of all of AIDS victims are women and children. Programs such as the President's Emergency Plan for AIDS Relief (PEPFAR), started by George W. Bush, have reduced the spread of the disease and helped its victims.[9]

Private charities and individual philanthropists have also made enormous contributions. For example, Paul Hewson, commonly known as Bono, is the singer of the Irish rock band U2. As a philanthropist, Bono has donated and facilitated donations of tens of millions of dollars to combat poverty and disease, especially in Africa. His fundraising work is made possible by economic free-dom—that's what makes Western countries wealthy, and wealthy countries have the means to aid poor countries.

While the United States is the global leader in humanitarian aid to Africa, China has focused on extracting oil and minerals from the continent, though it has also become a major builder of infrastructure projects. Even its aid programs focus on obtaining natural resources. China's actions represent a dark, alternative role for Africa than the one America is struggling to create through foreign aid. Instead of encouraging emerging democracies and healthy populations, China is pushing Africa in a direction where humanitarian aid is a mere afterthought to the voracious pursuit of oil and minerals.

China and the Debt Crisis

Currently, around $3.7 trillion in U.S. Treasury securities is foreign-owned. This is not necessarily bad; foreigners consider the U.S. government, supported by the richest economy in the world, to be a safe place to invest. The problem is that many of our major competitors, and in some cases, our adversaries, are buying our debt. This creates the possibility of countries trying to influence U.S. policy by threatening to stop buying our securities or to sell what they already own, which could raise interest rates and slow economic growth. While dumping U.S. Treasuries, a country could also sell dollars, which could weaken our currency, raise the price of imports, and stoke inflation. Our trade and budget deficits, along with our dependence on foreign oil, make the U.S. vulnerable to these financial pressures.

China is roughly tied with Japan as America's biggest creditor. Holding around $900 billion in treasuries,[10] China is one of our chief international competitors. If the rivalry between the two nations were to heat up, China would be in a strong position to blackmail or damage America by manipulating our debt. It's unsurprising that China is among our largest creditors. China accounts for some 18 percent of our imports but only about 7 percent of our exports.[11] The Chinese invest the dollars they earn from us in U.S. Treasuries and other assets, giving them crucial leverage over us in the event of future tensions.

In *The Tragedy of Great Power Politics*, political scientist John Mearsheimer argued, "The most dangerous states in the international system are continental powers with large armies." As national security expert Robert Kaplan notes, "This might be reason to fear China's influence as the country becomes more of a continental power. But China only partially fits Mearsheimer's description: its army, 1.6 million strong, is the largest in the world, but it will not have an expeditionary capability for years to come."[12] This reassuring notion, however, may not hold true for long. With the Chinese owning so much debt and investing heavily abroad to secure natural resources, they will eventually be in position to force countries to sell them expeditionary capability or simply form joint production capabilities with defense companies.

China will pose a major challenge to the United States for the foreseeable future. The country has simmering social instability related to its one child policy, to widespread corruption among local officials, and to crushing rural poverty. The Communist government can only keep a lid on these tensions through dictatorial police state tactics. This means China is unlikely to evolve into a friendly democracy, even as its economy becomes more capitalist.

In addition to China, the United States is also heavily indebted to oil exporting countries, many of which are hostile to our interests, including Venezuela, Iran, Saudi Arabia, and Libya. Combined, oil exporters are the fourth largest holders of U.S. debt. In fact, of the top ten countries holding U.S. Treasuries, only Britain, Japan, and Taiwan are long-standing, major allies.[13]

SOLUTION

The first step to dealing with our international challenges is to put our fiscal house in order. And we must act together and act quickly, because we're running out of time.

Countries rarely surrender when they are strong enough to win. Today, freedom's betrayal comes in the form of energy dependence, budget deficits, spiraling debt, and the unfunded liabilities of The Big Three. These challenges could achieve what Hitler, Stalin, the Kaiser, and George III couldn't bring about: the defeat of America.

We need to speak out for the beleaguered opponents of Hugo Chavez; support the Iranian people against their totalitarian government; destroy radical Islam; continue to offer hope to Africa through humanitarian aid; and out-compete the Communist Chinese. But all these efforts are complicated by America's precarious fiscal situation; there's not much point taking on all these challenges only to see the American economy collapse. And our rivals and enemies, of course, know full well where our weaknesses are, and they craft their strategies accordingly.

The American Roadmap offers real solutions. We must enact entitlement and tax reform in order to balance the budget and pay down our national debt—this will end our dangerous habit of borrowing from foreign governments. Likewise, the Energy Roadmap will reduce our dependence on foreign oil, cut our trade deficit in half, and allow us to stop financing Islamic extremists. Failure to act is not only irresponsible, but indeed reckless. As Admiral Hyman Rickover, the father of nuclear energy in America, had framed on his office wall,

"Our doubts are traitors and make us lose the good we oft might win by fearing to attempt."[14]

America must continue to spread liberty and democracy, for our own security and for the sake of the free world. But if we don't enact these reforms, we won't be able to spend a fraction of the resources we need for national security. Unless we resolve our critical fiscal problems, America's role in the world will be diminished—dramatically and permanently. As President Obama's economic advisor Larry Summers asked, "How long can the world's biggest borrower remain the world's biggest power?"[15]

No one else can help us with this task: our European allies are suffering the effects of decades of socialism such as low birthrates, economic stagnation, inflexible labor markets, and unsustainable deficits. The current European debt crisis should serve as a warning. After years of running up huge budget deficits to finance extensive social programs and a bloated public sector workforce, Europe's so-called PIGS—Portugal, Ireland, Greece, and Spain—are facing a reckoning. Paralyzed by financial crisis, Greece will only avoid the financial catastrophe of default through an international bailout. Meanwhile, Spain and Portugal received a shot across the bow when their debt was downgraded by a major rating agency. Observers are beginning to note that America, with our unprecedented deficits and massive national debt, is moving in the same direction—toward national insolvency.[16] The difference between us and the PIGS is that if the American economy goes under, there will be no one to bail us out.

Martin Luther King Jr. once said,

"The hottest place in Hell is reserved for those who remain neutral in times of great moral conflict."

The world needs our leadership. A weak America encourages our adversaries and will make the world a darker place. Our Republic must always be prepared to defend the blessings of liberty at home and, when necessary, abroad. There is no other country that can do it. That is why we must restore fiscal solvency. Otherwise, freedom could be betrayed once more, and for the last time.

CONCLUSION

"America is a shining city upon a hill whose beacon light guides freedom-loving people everywhere."
—President Ronald Reagan

THIS BOOK HAS OUTLINED REAL SOLUTIONS TO THE MOST SERIOUS problems facing our country—problems that threaten to turn America into a failed state. The threat is really that grave; when a country owes and spends more than it produces, when it is rich in resources but imports them from hostile countries, when its politicians no longer serve the people but only themselves—that nation will fail.

It's up to the citizens of our Republic to prevent this from happening. Americans must demand their representatives offer concrete solutions, not empty political rhetoric. The responsibility rests with you, whenever you vote. Everyday people elect Congress to write the laws and to change the laws when they don't work properly. So judge politicians not by what they say, but by what they do. If you want to know what a congressman believes, ask for his ideas in writing—preferably in legislative text—and hold him accountable on Election Day.

Although time is short, it's not too late. When enough politicians are elected who support the legislation outlined in this book, or perhaps come up with better ideas, our Republic can be restored. To pass legislation, it takes 218 votes in the House, either 51 or 60 votes in the Senate (depending on the opposition's tactics), and a president willing to sign the bill into law.

There's an old saying Washington politicians live by when they're asked for a commitment to do something. It goes like this:

"If you don't have to put it in writing, say it; if you don't have to say it, just nod your head yes; if you don't have to nod your head, wink; if you don't have to wink, simply stare."

Don't let your elected officials "stare" at you; get their solutions in writing.

Unafraid to put their ideas in writing, our Founding Fathers created the Constitution, one of the greatest documents in world history. This has led to the development of the most free and prosperous country in the world. As President Reagan beautifully described it:

"America is a shining city upon a hill whose beacon light guides freedom-loving people everywhere."

He continued this theme in his farewell address:

Let us resolve tonight that young Americans will always find there a city of hope in a country that is free. And let us resolve they will say of our day and our generation, we did keep the faith with our God, that we did act worthy of ourselves, that we did protect and pass on lovingly that shining city on a hill.

Millions of souls across the globe have seen this light, found hope, and were led from the ashes of despair.

Americans have always tried to share our values with people who sought the blessing of freedom. We have even sacrificed American lives to guarantee the survival of these values around the world. And now we must sacrifice once again to secure the blessings of life, liberty, and the pursuit of happiness. But this time, it is not in some far corner of the world, but here in America where we have to save ourselves from our own government.

Our Republic, a bastion of freedom in the world, is being systematically destroyed as radical ideologies replace the concept of limited government so cherished by the Founding Fathers. Communism isn't dead; it's just taken on new forms. Marxists, Maoists, socialists, fascists, and now radical environmentalists all have one common denominator: they seek to centralize and enhance government power in order to control the people.

The fate of the San Joaquin Valley, where I come from, offers a glimpse of America's grim future if we continue our current trajectory. There, the radical left and big government combined to take a real-life Garden of Eden—a region with some of the most fertile farmland in the world—and reduce it to a blighted, drought-stricken calamity. It's a tragic story that is playing out throughout the state of California, as utopian socialists hollow out the world's seventh largest economy.

It's a sad irony that the San Joaquin Valley today resembles the Dust Bowl, since the valley became famous as a lush place where Americans fled the actual Dust Bowl of the 1930s. In 1931, a severe drought hit Middle America, spreading in a few years to engulf the Oklahoma panhandle and a third of the Great Plains.

Thousands of people fled the region—many traveling to California along Route 66, which John Steinbeck called "the mother road, the road of flight" in *The Grapes of Wrath.*

Residents of the Great Plains fled west to escape the devastation of the Dust Bowl. (Photo by Dorothea Lange, courtesy of Library of Congress, Farm Security Administration - Office of War Information Photograph Collection)

Many of these "Okies" settled in the San Joaquin Valley, which had traditionally been a place where someone with few belongings, little education, and even no ability to speak English could prosper by picking grapes, milking cows, or hoeing cotton fields. The Oakies lived there alongside Portuguese, Mexican, Armenian, Italian, Basque, and Dutch immigrants. More recent arrivals in the valley hail from El Salvador, Vietnam, and India. I myself descend from a Portuguese family that came to the valley decades ago.

Early settlers worked with state and federal officials to build advanced irrigation systems that were the envy of the world. This included 1,200 miles of canals and nearly fifty reservoirs—a system that captured enough water to irrigate about 4 million acres and provide water to 23 million people. Combined with the fertile soil and ideal climate, the water helped to make the valley the world's most productive agricultural region.

That is, until radical environmentalists ruined the valley in a failed attempt to create a socialist utopia. It started in the 1990s, when ever-stricter regulations began to destroy the once-robust timber industry. President Clinton then put the San Joaquin Valley's few remaining timber areas off limits by declaring them a national monument. Mind you, we're not talking about Mount Rushmore here—we're talking about trees that for decades had been felled for timber and then replanted. Today the valley has just a single remaining mill, which only operates part-time. Meanwhile, both state and federal air quality regulations drove out much of the valley's industry, including our once-thriving trucking businesses.

The damage done by the timber and air regulations, however, paled in comparison to the harm that befell the valley when the environmental lobby declared war on our water supply. Americans outside California have a hard time believing it, but our government is denying water to its citizens, a policy usually only found in failed states like Robert Mugabe's Zimbabwe.

The first blow came in 1992 when Congress passed the Miller-Bradley Act, which diverted more than a million acre-feet of water from farmers to environmental projects and wildlife refuges. In succeeding years, state environmental regulations put even more water off-limits to agriculture. Finally, radical environmentalists, citing the Endangered Species Act, have won numerous lawsuits to restrict water usage even more in order to "protect" California's fish. Just since 2009, hundreds of billions of gallons of California's water, desperately needed by parched farmers, have been flushed under the Golden Gate Bridge to protect fish species including, infamously, the Delta smelt—a three-inch bait fish.

In nearly four decades, over 130 species of fish in California have been added to the endangered species list, while not a single fish has been removed. Simple logic would dictate that if years of increasing water flows for the exclusive use of fish have not solved the problem, then perhaps a new approach is needed.

Unfortunately, logic does not guide the twisted vision of radical environmentalists and their supporters in Congress. Opposing farming, industry, and nearly all other economic activity, green utopians want the San Joaquin Valley to revert back to a desert—and they're achieving their goal. Farmers are being systematically impoverished and uprooted as if they're enemies of the state. Mr. Mugabe, are you taking notes?

The valley's government-created Dust Bowl, where hundreds of thousands of acres of fertile land now lie fallow, has stunned local families. The government has chosen fish over them. And of course, the farmers' plight has damaged stores, restaurants, and many other local businesses that depend on agriculture, pushing the unemployment rate in the valley to nearly 20 percent. These families, many first, second, and third generation immigrants who fled to America to escape despots, dictators, Communism, and genocide, do not know how to respond. This is not the "shining city on the hill" their families cherished.

One small incident recently brought home to me the way the San Joaquin Valley has changed since I was a kid. One afternoon

Farmers and farm workers furious with the government-created drought erected protest signs in summer 2009.

in late summer 2009, I was walking through the dusty farm town of Mendota, where unemployment reaches 40 percent. Passing by an old house, I saw grown men sleeping in a flowerbed. The sight triggered a memory. When I was a kid, I would cool off by resting in the flowerbed after working in the fields. Yet these men weren't sleeping in flowerbeds for fun. Talking to them, I learned they were lying in the cool, damp dirt to escape the 100-degree heat because they were unemployed and their electricity had been turned off.

Congress has the power to solve this crisis—but it won't. In 2003, a fish-versus-families debate erupted in New Mexico after water deliveries to Albuquerque from the Rio Grande River were cut off to protect the silvery minnow—another three-inch bait fish. The Mayor of Albuquerque said at the time:

"The fringe environmental community, which wants to take away this city's destiny, wants to take water from the mouths of our children, will not prevail, not as long as I am in office."[1]

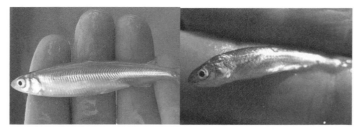

The Delta smelt (left) and the silvery minnow (right) are virtually identical. Smelt are abundant throughout the United States. (Photo by Aimee Roberson, U.S. Fish and Wildlife Service [left])

Congress moved quickly to suspend portions of the Endangered Species Act and let the water flow back to Albuquerque. The situation in California is identical, but Congress won't help—the environmental lobby has become too powerful. There simply are not 218 House members or 51 senators willing to cross the lobby for the sake of some powerless farmers in California. Worse still, the Democrats are using the manufactured water crisis to pry votes out of their own congressmen; just days before the vote on President Obama's healthcare bill, the administration agreed to increase the water supply in the San Joaquin Valley around the same time that two Democratic congressmen there promised to vote for the bill. As *Washington Post* columnist George Will noted:

> *Government policy having helped make water scarce in California's Central Valley, the party of expanding government secured two votes by increasing rations of the scarcity. Thus did one dependency lubricate legislation that establishes others.*[2]

The congressmen had little choice when confronted with an administration willing to cynically exploit their desperation to relieve the man-made drought. Sadly, the increased water ration they received—a boost from 5 percent to 25 percent of the valley's allocation—won't even provide minor relief. The drought will still be severe in the valley, meaning the administration can offer these congressmen more water in the future if their votes are needed again.

After the government had ignored the man-made drought for nine months as the San Joaquin Valley shed 20,000 jobs—a figure projected to rise to 80,000 if the drought continues—in autumn 2009 I went to a public meeting at the Department of the Interior to discuss the crisis. In front of local, state, and federal officials, along with members of Congress, I exclaimed:

"The people that pick the food are in a food line waiting for food. And do you know where the food came from? Carrots imported from China! For God's sake, what is wrong with this government?"

A food bank in Fresno County, California. The largest farm area in the world is importing Chinese carrots.

You may wonder what ultimately motivates the so-called environmentalists who have seized so much power in the San Joaquin Valley and are using it to completely restructure the way of life there. We get a hint from an observation by French philosopher Jean-Francois Revel, an ardent opponent of Communism who once remarked:

"Clearly, a civilization that feels guilty for everything it is and does will lack the energy and conviction to defend itself."[3]

Revel could have been describing the environmental lobby and other radical leftist groups today. Radicals always profess guilt over U.S. political and economic history. They take no pride in our civilization, even though it has produced unprecedented wealth, eradicated scores of diseases, increased life expectancy, educated millions, and raised the standard of living not only for generations of Americans but for many others around the world. Radical leftists will never defend what they do not believe in—and what they do not believe in, they will try to destroy.

God has blessed our country with abundant farmland that has made America self-sufficient in food production. Despite this luxury, radical environmentalists prefer to use the levers of big government to deprive whole communities of water and food in order to create a godless green utopia. Big business, which you might think would have resisted these attacks, instead tried to appease the radicals and was driven out of the valley long ago.

The fate of the San Joaquin Valley is being replicated throughout California. But those who are killing our food supply, depriving us of water, and driving out industry have ambitions that are not limited to my home state. The environmental lobby is a national effort, and they aim to use the ultimate big government—the one in Washington, D.C.—to impose their destructive notion of environmental virtue on the entire American people. What's more, their efforts are often assisted by big business, which frequently perceives that massive green programs and intrusive regulations, even if they're supposedly aimed at big business itself, can be gamed to its own advantage.

California's preventable crisis is no secret, but Americans from other states tend to dismiss it as an isolated situation; some neighboring states even benefit from the flow of people and business out of my home state. These Americans simply don't understand the danger they face—that the environmental extremism and suffocating regulation now sinking California will soon come to them. It all reminds me of an old poem about the rise of fascism written by the German pastor Martin Niemoller. To paraphrase his words:

> First they came for the loggers, and I did not speak out—because I was not a logger;
> Then they came for the truckers, and I did not speak out—because I was not a trucker;
> Then they came for the farmworkers, and I did not speak out—because I was not a farmworker;
> Then they came for the farmers, and I did not speak out—because I was not a farmer;
> Then they came for me—and there was no one left to speak out for me.

The victims of the left's senseless utopianism will be the American people. They never volunteered to have their lives turned upside down, to have their farms and industry destroyed along with millions of jobs, and to be banned from using their own natural resources. But that is exactly what the environmental lobby has in store for them. The San Joaquin Valley was a guinea pig in the greens' socialist experiment. Most people would consider the results disastrous, but for them, the more inhospitable the land becomes, the closer they come to realizing their strange dreamworld in which the land is no longer despoiled by humans growing anything or building anything.

.   .   .

Although I am a conservative, I have avoided using that term in this book. The reason is simple: conservative has come to mean different things to different people. Rarely is the question asked: what exactly is a conservative and what is it that they want to conserve? For to be a conservative, you must believe in conserving something. My goal is to conserve our Republic by protecting the liberties of the individual—because it is through the empowerment of individuals that we create the enduring bond that holds our Republic together.

At the close of the Constitutional Convention of 1787, as Benjamin Franklin was leaving Independence Hall in Philadelphia, a lady stopped and asked him:

"*Well, Doctor, what have we got—a Republic or a Monarchy?*"

Franklin replied, "*A Republic, if you can keep it.*"

ACKNOWLEDGMENTS

THIS BOOK WOULD NOT HAVE BEEN POSSIBLE WITHOUT MY EDITOR, Dr. Jack Langer. I'd also like to thank my many friends and family who took time to read the book in its early stages and who gave me faith that I was doing something worthwhile.

NOTES

Introduction

1   Letters from *Thomas Jefferson to Isaac Weaver*, June 1807;
    available at:
    http://etext.virginia.edu/jefferson/quotations/jeff0600.htm.
2   Ibid.
3   Steve Milloy, *Green Hell* (Washington, D.C.: Regnery
    Publishing, 2009), 170.
4   See: http://www.newsmeat.com/ceo_political_donations/
    Henry_Paulson.php.
5   Thomas Jefferson to T. B. Hollis, 1787; available at:
    http://etext.virginia.edu/jefferson/quotations/jeff0600.htm.

Chapter One

1 Laura Blumenfeld, "The $700 billion man," *The Washington Post*, December 6, 2009; available at: http://www.washingtonpost.com/wp-dyn/content/article/2009/12/04/AR2009120402016.html.

2 Newt Gingrich, *To Save America* (Washington, D.C.: Regnery, 2010), 87.

3 "Obamacare: It's Not Getting Better," The Heritage Foundation, March 15, 2010; available at: http://www.heritage.org/Research/Factsheets/Obamacare-It-s-Not-Getting-Better.

4 Ricardo Alonso Zaldivar, "Report says health care will cover more, cost more," Associated Press, April 23, 2010; article previously available at: http://www.washingtonpost.com/wp-dyn/content/article/2010/04/23/AR2010042300843.html; article currently available at: http://news.yahoo.com/s/ap/20100423/ap_on_bi_ge/us_health_care_law_costs.

Chapter Two

1 Kimberly A. Strassel, "The Greens' Ground Zero," *Wall Street Journal*, April 16, 2010; available at: http://online.wsj.com/article/SB10001424052702304510004575186392195182342.html.

2 *The Orange County Register*, August 26, 2001; information available at: http://archive.fairvote.org/redistricting/reports/remanual/canews4.htm.

3   Ibid.

4   See David Freddoso, "C-Span's Lamb: Obama used us as a political football," *Washington Examiner*, January 7, 2010; available at: http://www.washingtonexaminer.com/opinion/blogs/ beltway-confidential/C-Spans-Lamb-Obama-used-us-as-a- political-football-80909722.html.

Chapter Three

1   Energy Information Administration, Energy Consumption by Primary Energy Source, Selected Years, 1949-2008; available at: http://www.eia.doe.gov/emeu/aer/pdf/pages/sec1_9.pdf.

2   Energy Information Administration, Energy Consumption by Energy Source, Selected Years, 2004-8; available at: http://www.eia.doe.gov/cneaf/alternate/page/renew_ener- gy_consump/table1.html.

3   Gene Whitney, Carl E. Behrens, and Carol Glover, "U.S. Fossil Fuel Resources: Terminology, Reporting, and Summary," Congressional Research Service, October 28, 2009; available at: http://epw.senate.gov/public/index.cfm?FuseAction= Files.View&FileStore_id=f7bd7b77-ba50-48c2-a635- 220d7cf8c519.

4   "Issue Focus: Oil and Gas Leasing on Federal Lands," June 25, 2008; available at: http://www.instituteforenergyre- search.org/2008/06/25/ truth-about-ocs/.

5   Quoted in *National Geographic* (Energy Report), February 1981.

6   BBC News, Interview with Dr. Gerd Leipold, August 4, 2009; available at: http://news.bbc.co.uk/2/hi/programmes/hardtalk/8184392.stm.

7   David M. Graber, "Mother Nature as a Hothouse Flower," *Los Angeles Times*, October 22, 1989; available at: http://articles.latimes.com/1989-10-22/books/bk-726_1_bill-mckibben/3, p. 3.

8   Patrick Moore, "Going Nuclear," *The Washington Post*, April 16, 2006; available at: http://www.washingtonpost.com/wp-dyn/content/article/2006/04/14/AR2006041401209.html.

9   Energy & the Environment Myths & Facts, Myth 10; available at: http://www.manhattan-institute.org/energymyths/myth10.htm.

10   Joanne Nova, "Climate Money," Science and Public Policy Institute, July 21, 2009; available at: http://scienceandpublicpolicy.org/images/stories/papers/originals/climate_money.pdf.

11   "Q&A: Professor Phil Jones," BBC News, February 13, 2010; available at: http://news.bbc.co.uk/2/hi/8511670.stm.

12   Juliet Eilperin, "Hackers steal electronic data from top climate research center," *The Washington Post*, November 21, 2009; available at: http://www.washingtonpost.com/wp-dyn/content/article/2009/11/20/AR2009112004093.html.

13   For a primer on UN corruption, see the account of reporter Claudia Rossett's 2009 speech on the Oil for Food scandal and other instances of UN malfeasance: Jerry Gordon, "Claudia Rossett: The UN Is Absolutely Corrupt," *New English Review*, February 2009; available at: http://www.newenglishreview.org/custpage.cfm/frm/32207/sec_id/32207.

14 "Al Gore Could Become World's First Carbon Billionaire,"
    The Telegraph, November 3, 2009;
    http://www.telegraph.co.uk/earth/energy/6491195/Al-
    Gore-could-become-worlds-first-carbon-billionaire.html.

15 "Gore's 'carbon offsets' Paid to Firm he Owns," *Worldnet
    Daily News*, March 2, 2007; available at:
    http://www.wnd.com/?pageId=40445.

16 U.S. Timber Production, Trade, and Consumption and Price
    Statistics 1965-2005, U.S. Department of Agriculture,
    September 2007.

17 Data available at:
    http://evergreenmagazine.com/pages/Forest_Facts-v2.html.

18 Michael Fumento, "How to Save Endangered Species: As
    Costs Soar, Markets May Be the Best Tool"; available at:
    http://fumento.com/economy/endangered.html.

19 U.S. Fish & Wildlife Service, "Recovery Plan for the
    Northern Spotted Owl," May 2008; available at:
    http://www.fws.gov/Pacific/ecoservices/endangered/recov-
    ery/pdf/NSO%20Final%20Rec%20Plan%20051408.pdf.

20 Francie Grace, "Blasting Some Owls To Save Others?" CBS
    News, April 27, 2007; available at:
    http://www.cbsnews.com/stories/2007/04/27/tech/main273
    6996.shtml.

21 Joshua Kurlantzick, "Put a Tyrant in Your Tank," *Mother
    Jones*, May/June 2008; available at:
    http://motherjones.com/environment/2008/05/put-tyrant-
    your-tank.

22 Stephen Power and Ben Casselman, "Defections Shake Up
    Climate Coalition," *Wall Street Journal*, February 17, 2010;
    available at:

http://online.wsj.com/article/SB1000142405274870480420
4575069440096420212.html.

23   Opinion, "Obama Underwrites Offshore Drilling," *Wall Street Journal*, August 18, 2009; available at: http://online.wsj.com/article/SB1000142405297020386320
4574346610120524166.html.

24   Country Energy Profiles, Energy Information Administration; available at: http://tonto.eia.doe.gov/country/index.cfm.

25   "China, Cuba reported in Gulf oil partnership," CNN Money, May 9, 2006; available at: http://money.cnn.com/2006/05/09/news/economy/oil_cuba/index.htm.

26   David Pierson, "China's push for oil in Gulf of Mexico puts U.S. in awkward spot," *Los Angeles Times*, October 22, 2009; available at: http://articles.latimes.com/2009/oct/22/business/fi-china-oil22.

27   Energy Information Administration, "U.S. Imports by Country of Origin," http://tonto.eia.doe.gov/dnav/pet/pet_move_impcus_a2_nus_ep00_im0_mbblpd_m.htm; "Energy Overview," http://www.eia.doe.gov/emeu/aer/overview.html.

28   Alaska Department of Fish and Game, Caribou; available at: http://www.adfg.state.ak.us/pubs/notebook/biggame/caribou.php.

29   Arctic Power, Anwar Information Brief, http://www.anwar.org/features/pdfs/caribou-facts.pdf; and "Co-existing with oil development, Central Arctic caribou herd thrives, population at record highs" http://www.anwr.org/images/pdf/Cariboufinal_6-09.pdf.

30   Alaska Department of Fish and Game, Caribou; available at: http://www.adfg.state.ak.us/pubs/notebook/biggame/caribou.php.

31   Coca Cola Company/Polar Bear Support Fund, http://polarbears.thecoca-colacompany.com/polarbear supportfund/about/.

32   Kenneth P. Green, "Polar Bear Risk Claims on Thin Ice," American Enterprise Institute, May 9, 2008; available at: http://www.aei.org/article/27971; James Delingpole, "Polar Bears In Danger? Is That Some Kind Of Joke?" *UK Times*, November 12, 2007; available at: http://www.timesonline.co.uk/tol/comment/columnists/gues t_contributors/article2852551.ece.

33   Michael Lynch, "Obama misses the big oil," *New York Times*, April 4, 2010; available at: http://www.nytimes.com/2010/04/05/opinion/05lynch.html.

34   "Offshore Drilling: Democrats Urge Halt to New Wells, Push for Spill Investigations," *Environment and Energy Publishing*, April 29, 2010.

35   "Scuttle the USS Murtha," *The Weekly Standard*, May 10, 2010; available at: http://www.weeklystandard.com/articles/scuttle-uss-murtha?page=2.

36   Michael Lynch, "Obama misses the big oil," *New York Times*, April 4, 2010; available at: http://www.nytimes.com/2010/04/05/opinion/05lynch.html.

37   Theodore Rockwell, *The Rickover Effect: How One Man Made A Difference*, An Authors Guild Backinprint.com edition, 2002.

38 Theodore Rockwell, *Creating a New World: Stories & Images from the Dawn of the Atomic Age*, 2nd edition (1st Books Library, 2004).

39 Oil Shale and Tar Sands Programmatic EIS, http://www.ostseis.anl.gov/guide/oilshale/index.cfm.

40 "Czech President Klaus: Global Warming Not Science, but a 'New Religion,'" FOX News, December 18, 2009; available at: http://www.foxnews.com/scitech/2009/12/18/czech-president-klaus-global-warming-science-new-religion/.

Chapter Four

1 Kaiser Family Foundation Publication #7305-04, Figure 5, "Estimated Sources of Medicare Revenue, 2010"; available at: http://facts.kff.org/chart.aspx?ch=380.

2 Life Expectancy in the United States, Table 1, Library of Congress / Congressional Research Service #RL32792; available at: http://aging.senate.gov/crs/aging1.pdf.

3 2009 Annual Report of the Social Security Board of the Trustees; available at: http://www.ssa.gov/OACT/TRSUM/index.html.

4 Committee on Ways and Means, Hearing Transcript from May 12, 2005; Serial 109-22; available at: http://waysand-means.house.gov/hearings/transcript.aspx?newsid=10134.

5 Kaiser Family Foundation Medicaid and State Funded Coverage Income Eligibility Limits for Low-Income Adults, 2009; available at: http://www.statehealthfacts.org/comparereport.jsp?rep=54& cat=4.

6   Kathryn Nix, "Obamacare: Impact on the Uninsured," The
    Heritage Foundation, April 20, 2010; available at:
    http://www.heritage.org/Research/Reports/2010/04/Obama
    care-Impact-on-the-Uninsured.

7   Karen Davis and Sara R. Collins, "Medicare at Forty,"
    CMS: Health Care Financing Review / Winter 2005-2006,
    Volume 27, Number 2; available at:
    http://www2.cms.gov/HealthCareFinancingReview/down-
    loads/05-06Winpg53.pdf.

8   "Life Expectancy in the United States," Table 1 Library of
    Congress / Congressional Research Service #RL32792;
    available at: http://aging.senate.gov/crs/aging1.pdf.

9   2009 Annual Report of the Federal Hospital Insurance
    Trust Funds Figure II, E2; available at:
    www.cms.gov/reportstrustfunds/downloads/tr2009.pdf, p. 19.

10 See footnote 16, chapter 4.

11 Ricardo Alonso-Zaldivar, "Report says health care will cover
    more, cost more," Associated Press; article previously avail-
    able at: http://www.washingtonpost.com/wp-
    dyn/content/article/2010/04/23/AR2010042300843.html;
    available at:
    http://abcnews.go.com/Business/wireStory?id=10454567.

12 Lyndon Baines Johnson Library and Museum White House
    telephone conversations archive Citation No.: 7141, Tape:
    WH6503.11, Program: 9; available at:
    www.lbjlib.utexas.edu/johnson/archives.hom/dictabelt.hom/
    content.asp.

13 Ibid.

14 The Congressional Record House, April 8, 1965, Page 7435.

15 Office of Management and Budget, The President's Budget, Historic Tables: Table 3.1, www.thewhitehouse.gov/omb/budget/historicals.

16 U.S. Treasury Department, *2009 Financial Report of the U.S. Government Note 26*; available at: http://www.fms.treas.gov/fr/09frusg/09frusg.pdf; "Mandatory Spending Since 1962," Library of Congress/ Congressional Research Service; available at: http://www.crs.gov/ReportPDF/RL33074.pdf.

Chapter Five

1 Scott A. Hodge, "Record Numbers of People Paying No Income Tax; Over 50 Million 'Nonpayers' Include Families Making over $50,000," Tax Foundation Fiscal Fact No. 214, March 10, 2010; available at: http://www.taxfoundation.org/publications/show/25962.ht ml; see also Robert Willimas, "Who Pays No Income Tax?" Tax Policy Center Tax Facts; available at: http://www.tax-policycenter.org/UploadedPDF/ 1001289_who_pays.pdf.

2 Internal Revenue Service, "Tax Quotes"; available at: http://www.irs.gov/newsroom/article/0,,id=110483,00.html.

3 Tax Foundation, "Number of Words in Internal Revenue Code and Federal Tax Regulations, 1955-2005," October 26, 2006; available at: http://www.taxfoundation.org/research/show/1961.html.

4 "National Taxpayer Advocate Urges Tax Simplification and Compassionate Treatment of Taxpayers Hit by Recession,"

Internal Revenue Service, January 7, 2009; available at: http://www.irs.gov/newsroom/article/0,,id=202260,00.html.

5   Ibid.

6   Tax Foundation, "U.S. Federal Individual Income Tax Rates History, 1913-2010," December 31, 2009; available at: http://www.taxfoundation.org/files/fed_individual_rate_ history-20091231.pdf.

7   "The Debt to the Penny and Who Holds It," U.S. Department of the Treasury Bureau of the Public Debt; available at: http://www.treasurydirect.gov/NP/BPDLogin?application=np.

8   Office of Management and Budget, *Historical Tables* (Fiscal Year 2011); available at: http://www.whitehouse.gov/omb/budget/fy2011/assets/hist.pdf.

9   "Summary of Latest Federal Individual Income Tax Data," Tax Foundation, Fiscal Fact No. 183, July 30, 2009; available at: http://www.taxfoundation.org/research/show/250.html.

10 William Ahern, "Can Income Tax Hikes Close the Deficit?" Fiscal Facts, March 12, 2010; available at: http://www.tax-foundation.org/files/ff217.pdf.

11 Steven C. Johnson and Leah Schnurr, "Volcker: Taxes likely to rise eventually to tame deficit," Reuters, April 6, 2010; available at: http://www.reuters.com/article/idUSTRE6355N520100406.

12 Charles Babington, "Obama suggests value-added tax may be an option," Associated Press, April 21, 2010; available at: http://news.yahoo.com/s/ap/20100421/ap_on_bi_ge/us_obama_tax.

13 See my blog for a link to the study by AEI, "You can't spend what you don't have. Let's try something new,"

October 13, 2009; available at:
http://devinnunes.blogspot.com/2009/10/you-cant-spend-what-you-dont-have-let.html.

Chapter Six

1   Chad C. Haddal, "Border Security: The Role of the U.S.
Border Patrol," Congressional Research Service, March 3,
2010 (R32562).

2   Editorial, "Mexico's drug violence respects no borders," *Los
Angeles Times*, January 5, 2010; available at:
http://articles.latimes.com/2010/jan/05/opinion/la-ed-mexico5-2010jan05.

Chapter Seven

1   U.S. Department of Education, National Center for Education
Statistics, Table 25. Expenditures of educational institution
related to the gross domestic product: selected years, 1929-
1930 through 2007-2008; Table ESE65, Enrollment in public
elementary and secondary schools, by level, grade, and jurisdic-
tion 1965; and Public Elementary and Secondary School
Students Enrollment and Staff from school year 2007.

2   U.S. Department of Education, National Center for
Education Statistics, Common Core of Data 2006-2007.

3   U.S. Department of Education, National Center for
Education Statistics, Common Core of Data 2006-2007;
U.S. Department of Education, Ten Facts about K-12
Education Funding; Editorial Projects in Education,
Research Center Maps, School District Graduation Reports
(www.edweek.org/apps/gmap).

4   Editorial Projects in Education, Research Center Maps,
    School District Graduation Reports
    (www.edweek.org/apps/gmap); U.S. Department of
    Education, Center for Education Statistics, Common Core
    of Data 2006-2007.

5   U.S. Department of Education, National Center for
    Education Statistics, Common Core of Data 2006-2007.

6   Editorial Projects in Education, Research Center Maps,
    School District Graduation Reports
    (www.edweek.org/apps/gmap); U.S. Department of
    Education, Center for Education Statistics, Common Core
    of Data 2006-2007.

7   Richard Leiby, "Obama Girls Will Go to Sidwell Friends,"
    The Washington Post, November 22, 2008; available at:
    http://www.washingtonpost.com/wp-dyn/content/arti-
    cle/2008/11/21/AR2008112103248.html.

8   Editorial, "Presumed Dead," *The Washington Post*, April 11,
    2009; available at: http://www.washingtonpost.com/wp-
    dyn/content/article/2009/04/10/AR2009041003073.html.

9   Neal McCluskey, "Retiring General Counsel's Shocking
    Admission: The NEA is a Union!" the Cato Institute, July
    10, 2009; available at: http://www.cato-at-
    liberty.org/2009/07/10/retiring-general-counsels-shocking-
    admission-the-nea-is-a-union/.

10 U.S. Department of Education, National Center for Education
    Statistics, National Assessment of Educational Progress.

11 U.S. Department of Education, Ten Facts about K-12
    Education Funding.

12 Heritage Foundation Survey, Chart 1 B 2257, March 13, 2009.

Chapter Eight

1   The (U.S.) National Archives; available at: http://www.archives.gov/exhibits/treasures_of_congress/text/page8_text.html.

2   Naval History & Heritage Command; available at: http://www.history.navy.mil/photos/events/wwii-pac/pearlhbr/pearlhbr.htm.

3   Lisa Beyer et al., "After 9: Saudi Arabia: inside the kingdom," *Time*, September 15, 2003; available at: http://www.time.com/time/magazine/article/0,9171,1005663-8,00.html.

4   "Saudi Publications On Hate Ideology Invade American Mosques," Freedom House, Center for Religious Freedom; available at: http://www.freedomhouse.org/uploads/special_report/45.pdf.

5   National Drug Intelligence Center: Dept. of State.

6   "Chavez Under Fire From International Community," *Financial Times*, March 7, 2010; available at: http://www.ft.com/cms/s/0/4a01ef1e-29dd-11df-b940-00144feabdc0.html.

7   Ted Dagne, "Africa: U.S. Foreign Assistance Issues," Congressional Research Service, March 3, 2010 (RL33591).

8   USAID, "Sub-Saharan Africa"; available at: http://www.usaid.gov/locations/sub-saharan_africa/.

9   USAID, "HIV/AIDS"; available at: http://www.usaid.gov/our_work/global_health/aids/global-aids101.html.

10 "China's foreign reserves hit new high," *Bloomberg Business Week*, April 12, 2010; available at: http://www.business-week.com/ap/financialnews/D9F1GUTG0.htm.

11 United States Census Bureau, Top Trading Partners Total Trade, Exports, Imports; available at: http://www.census.gov/foreign-trade/statistics/highlights/top/top0912yr.html.

12 *Foreign Affairs*, May/Jun 2010, Vol 89, Issue 3, 22–41.

13 "Major Foreign Holders of Treasury Securities," U.S. Treasury; available at: http://www.ustreas.gov/tic/mfh.txt.

14 Theodore Rockwell, *Creating The New World* (1st Books Library, 2004), 102.

15 David E. Sanger, "Deficits may alter U.S. politics and global power," *New York Times*, February 1, 2010; available at: http://community.nytimes.com/comments/www.nytimes.com/2010/02/02/us/politics/02deficit.html.

16 Niall Ferguson, "A Greek Crisis Is Coming to America," *Financial Times*, February 10, 2010; article available at: http://www.businessinsider.com/a-greek-crisis-is-coming-to-america-2010-2.

Conclusion

1 *The Gazette* (Colorado Springs), June 18, 2003.

2 "A battle won, but a victory?" *The Washington Post*, March 23, 2010; available at: http://www.washingtonpost.com/wp-dyn/content/article/2010/03/22/AR2010032201528.html.

3 Quoted in Ambassador Jeane Kirkpatrick's speech to the 1984 Republican Convention.

INDEX